LA GLOIRE

*The Roman Empire of
Corneille and Racine*

LA GLOIRE

The Roman Empire of
Corneille and Racine

Louis Auchincloss

UNIVERSITY OF SOUTH CAROLINA PRESS

Published in Columbia, South Carolina, by the
University of South Carolina Press

Manufactured in the United States of America

00   99   98   97   96   5   4   3   2   1

Library of Congress Cataloging-in-Publication Data
Auchincloss, Louis.
    La gloire : the Roman Empire of Corneille and Racine / Louis
Auchincloss.
        p.   cm.
    ISBN 1–57003–122–3
    1. Corneille, Pierre, 1606–1684—Criticism and
interpretation.   2. Racine, Jean, 1639–1699—Criticism
and interpretation.   3. Rome—In literature.   I. Title.
PQ1772.A95   1996
842'.4093237—dc20   96–38634

For Martha Rusk Sutphen,
than whom Adele and I had no dearer friend.

CONTENTS

LA GLOIRE

The Roman Empire of
Corneille and Racine

.

INTRODUCTION

In modern times, though perhaps starting as far back as the historian Edward Gibbon (1737–1794), there is a tendency to think of the Roman Empire as a political entity in a condition of constant decline, a decadent slave state, always overrun by barbarians it was too effete to resist, with a population whose principal diversion was watching gladiatorial combats and Christians fed to the lions.

Yet to intellectuals of the seventeenth century the Roman Empire represented a culture and a civilization superior to any in their contemporary Europe. The statue of James II outside the National Gallery in London was clad in a toga; Latin was the language of scholars and diplomats, and Ceasar was the title of the Holy Roman Emperor who still claimed to rule the world. Roman law stood for order and justice, and Roman virtue was the ideal of the warrior.

France was then the great power of Europe. Louis XIV was more like Augustus than like any Hapsburg in Vienna, and the advance of the Roman legions to the mists of Scotland and the deserts of Parthia seemed a foreshadowing of the aggressive military policies of Richelieu and the Sun King. The millennium of Roman history from Romulus to Romulus Augustulus (753 B.C. to 476 A.D.) provided a rich source of themes for the classic tragedians of the day, replete as it was with glorious victories and triumphal marches. And it was equally well stocked with murders

1

and treacheries and usurpations. And love, too, of course, so necessary for the dramatist, though Venus was not apt to be a friendly goddess to those who found themselves in her talons.

The form of the French classic tragedy has always been a bit of a poser to non-Gallic audiences. Why must the action be limited to a single chamber, usually a room in a palace, and why must it all take place in twenty-four hours, all too ludicrously few, in most cases, for the events crammed into them? Why can there be no violence on the scene, no horseplay, no relieving comedy? Why must the language be limited to noble words? Do we really care about alternating masculine and feminine rhymes? It takes some time and considerable adaptation before the reader who has been (justly) raised to think Shakespeare the peerless playwright can adapt to the methods of Corneille and Racine. But when he or she has done so, the rewards are great indeed. For the limitations of a French tragedian enabled the playwright to cast a brilliant and remorseless beam of light on the crux of the problem to which he addressed himself and hold it there until understanding and catharsis were complete. This can give the reader or audience a unique aesthetic experience; it is poetry at its most intense.

Thus in *Horace* Corneille creates a vivid sense of the single red moment when patriotism explodes into madness, and in *Britannicus* Racine can select the exact time when the balance between the generosity of young Nero's nature and his latent sadism turns irrevocably in favor of the latter.

To read the plays, of course, is to see Rome through French eyes of a bygone period, but to look at one culture through the prism of another can lead to interesting discoveries about one's own. Questions of civic and military glory are hardly irrelevant to our own times. Unfortunately the plays must be read in French for any true appreciation of their essentially untranslatable beauty. The only poet who has had any degree of success in putting French classic drama into English—and he is remarkable—is Richard Wilbur, but to date he has done only Racine's *Andromaque* and *Phèdre*.

Pierre Corneille (1606–1684) and his younger theatrical rival,

Jean Racine (1639–1699), are often contrasted to each other, like two Tobey jars on different ends of a mantel. Corneille is seen as sterner and more heroic; his Romans and their subjects are obsessed with a lofty sense of duty to the family and state and tortured by bewildering conflicts of interest. Racine's characters, on the other hand, are more troubled by problems of the heart; they are the victims of a remorseless Venus.

Corneille, in a word, was the poet of patriotism, the celebrator of the military genius of France which had brought to the country national unity and international power, under the ministries of Richelieu and Mazarin and, in the poet's later years, in the reign of the young Louis XIV. He believed implicitly in absolute monarchy; any doubts that he might once have had, when suffering Richelieu's disapproval of *Le Cid,* were dispelled after he had made his peace with that great man. Nothing, even in his rank-revering century, could have been more stooping than his dedication of *Horace* to the cardinal. In that dedication Corneille wrote of his eminence attending a dramatic performance: "C'est là que lisant sur son visage ce qui lui plaît et ce qui ne lui plaît pas, nous nous instruisons avec certitude de ce qui est bon et ce qui est mauvais, et tirons des règles infaillibles de ce qu'il faut suivre et ce qu'il faut éviter; c'est là que j'ai souvent appris en deux heures ce que mes livres n'eussent pu m'apprendre en dix ans."[*]

Dictatorship, in Corneille's opinion, was the only way in which his nation could fulfill her manifest destiny. This destiny was defined by a character in his tragedy *Attila* who was gifted with a preview into the future of France:

> Mais si de nos devins l'oracle n'est point faux,
> Sa grandeur doit atteindre aux degrés les plus hauts;
> Et de ses successeurs l'empire inébranlable
> Sera de siècle en siècle enfin si redoutable,

---

[*]Thus gleaning from his features what pleases and what fails to please him, we learn with certitude what is good and what is bad, and deduce infallible rules as to what to follow and what to avoid. So I have often learned in two hours what my books couldn't have taught me in ten years.

Qu'un jour toute la terre en recevra des lois,
Ou tremblera du moins au nom de leurs François.*

Mark his use of the verb *trembler*. Corneille's concept of national greatness was always associated with the neighbors of France trembling in their boots. But the remarkable thing about him was that he made no bones about it. He saw the world as it was, violent and bloodthirsty, and pulled out of the mess such valor as he could find. Whatever one may think of his conclusions, his vision made for great poetry.

He had always been a student of the Roman Empire in which he saw a precursor of his own country. The long and glorious rise of the Eternal City and its long and less glorious decline gave him the material for no less than twelve tragedies, from the legendary, pre-historical Rome of *Horace* to the Byzantine empire of *Pulchérie* in the fifth century A.D. I shall take them up, not chronologically as they were written, but chronologically as the events they record occurred. We shall find our poet concerned with questions of patriotism, free will, political opportunism, self-sacrifice and self-aggrandisement, but above all with the question of "gloire."

Gloire might be defined as the lofty ideal that the hero (and more rarely the heroine) has set for himself and which he believes to be his destiny or mission in the world. *Gloire* must be maintained at all costs, whether of his own life or those of others, and no matter how many of the latter. That this may lead him to the ugliest acts of aggression and even murder may be regretted; that it may result in his being publicly berated as well as applauded may be unfortunate, but he can usually count on history to justify him. *Gloire* must prevail over the most passionate love of a woman, the closest friendship with a man, and even the closest family ties. It has struck me in reading these plays that some such concept may have given zeal to those of our Central Intelligence Agency who, though possessed of the keenest brains and highest

---

*But if the oracle of our priests be true, his greatness is destined to reach the heights, and the unshakable sway of his successors will render laws to all the world, or at least make the world tremble at the very name of Frenchmen.

character, allowed themselves to be drawn into plots to assassinate foreign dictators.

Racine, at least in our day and certainly outside of France, is far more popular than Corneille. He speaks more to the heart than to the mind, and intense patriotism, increasingly identified with ethnic divisions and national breakups, has become suspect to the thoughtful. Even in France the leading actresses have made greater names with Racine than with his sterner competitor; *Phèdre* is to them the test that *Hamlet* is to the British actor. The Racinian heroine is so driven by passion as to be hardly aware that her country's welfare may be at stake. Hermoine in *Andromaque* immolates the hero of the Greeks to her jealous rage; Roxane in *Bajazet* initiates a civil war to gain a lover; Phèdre in her eponymous tragedy allows the promising heir to the crown to go to his death to conceal her incestuous love.

Yet we shall see in the Roman plays that the two masters were capable of changing places. *Mithridate* is a "Louis XIV" drama; it might have come from the pen of Corneille, and *Suréna* has much of the pathos and sadness and resignation of Racine's *Bérénice*. But when they used the identical theme, as in *Bérénice* and Corneille's *Tite et Bérénice*, Racine prevailed, because the love that had to be sacrificed to the glory of Rome was more peculiarly his subject.

In the discussions that follow, all translations from the plays are by the author of this book.

Horace

I n *Horace* Corneille addressed himself to the question of *gloire* with greater candor and in more detail than in any of the other Roman plays. His plot faithfully follows Livy. According to legend the rival cities of Alba and Rome agreed to settle their differences and merge into a single nation under the rule of the one whose chosen team of three warriors should prevail in a mortal duel with the other's. Rome chose Horace and his two brothers; Alba, Curiace and his two. The situation is complicated in the play in that the families of the two teams are closely united by friendship, love, and marriage. Horace's wife, Sabine, is Curiace's sister, and Curiace is engaged to Horace's sister, Camille. And Horace and Curiace are best friends.

In the duel Horace's brothers are both killed, but he himself is unwounded while the three Alba brothers are all more or less badly hurt. By the ruse of fleeing and letting his three opponents pursue him at different speeds, Horace separates them and then dispatches them one by one. Returning home in the hot flush of victory he encounters his sister, Camille, who curses him and Rome for the slaughter of her betrothed. In a rage he kills her, but he is pardoned by the Roman king in consideration of his great victory.

It was a situation tailor-made for the poetic genius of Corneille. The nicely balancing conflicts of love and duty, family and country, loyalty and patriotism are debated in sparkling verse

7

with passionate pride and passionate woe. The play is like a glittering jewel being slowly turned at the end of a gold chain. But let us get to the question of *gloire*.

The poet makes it entirely clear that the city whose champions are defeated will not be in any way humiliated in the ensuing merger. Her citizens will take their proper place in the united empire,

> Mais sans indignité pour des guerriers si braves.
> Qu'ils deviennent sujets sans devenir esclaves,
> Sans honte, sans tribut, et sans autre rigueur
> Que de suivre en tous lieux les drapeaux du vainqueur.*

But that means nothing to Horace. To follow any flag but Rome's must be a disgrace which he has no wish to survive. He is jubilant when he learns that he and his brothers have been chosen to fight for their country. He will not allow his loving wife, Sabine, to shed a single tear over the risk he will be taking or the one equally incurred by her three brothers. He exclaims:

> Quoi? vous me pleureriez mourant pour mon pays!
> Pour un cœur généreux ce trépas a des charmes;
> La gloire qui le suit ne souffre point de larmes,
> Et je le recevrais en bénissant mon sort,
> Si Rome et tout l'état perdaient moins en ma mort.†

When his friend Curiace comes to deplore the grim doom of their approaching encounter, Horace won't hear of it as a disaster. If he dies in defeat he will not have to survive what he insists on seeing as his country's humiliation, and if he dies or survives in victory he will be equally happy. He sees, as I'm afraid a contemporary French audience would have seen, Curiace's only too human distress as the sign of a weakness which may be fatal in battle. At last he virtually turns his back on his friend:

---

*But without humiliation to warriors so valiant, they will beome subjects and not slaves, having only to follow, their dignity intact, the flag of the victors.

†What? You would pity me dying for my country! For a loyal heart such an end has only delight. The glory of it is beyond tears, and I should bless my fate if it spared Rome a loss.

Rome a choisi mon bras, je n'examine rien;
Avec une allégresse aussi pleine et sincère
Que j'épousai la sœur, je combattrai le frère;
Et pour trancher enfin ces discours superflus,
Albe vous a nommé, je ne vous connais plus.*

One cannot help but wonder if Corneille had read Shakespeare's play about a very similar hero, Coriolanus, who when asked by a fellow general in battle if he were not wounded, cheerfully replies:

O! let me clip ye
In arms as sound as when I woo'd, in heart
As merry as when our nuptial day was done,
And tapers burnt to bedward.

The joys of killing and loving must be equal to a hero.

Horace's sister forms a perfect balance to him. Camille, as charming in her weakness as he is repellent in his strength, is everything that he is not. Her love for Curiace consumes her. When an oracle gives her the false assurance that her lover will survive the duel, she is so wildly happy that her gay greeting of an old admirer convinces witnesses that she has changed her affections. And when she leaps to the absurdly mistaken conclusion that Curiace's unexpected presence in her home means that he has refused to take part in the coming duel, she assures him that whatever the world will think of such conduct, it will make him only the dearer to her. It is only to be expected, when she learns of her lover's death, and her father sternly forbids her to weep for her country's foe, that she should go half mad with grief and fury.

What Camille represents of human passion and weakness and what Horace stands for in human courage and hardness are bound to clash, and the result is wonderful theatre. But when Horace runs his sword through Camille—off stage, of course, as required by classical rules—I don't see how any audience can avoid loath-

---

*Rome has enlisted my arm in its defense; I look no further. With the same high joy that I felt in wedding the sister, I shall fight the brother. And to cut short this discussion, let me simply say: Alba has named you; I know you no longer.

ing him or his terrible old father. The question remains: how did Corneille feel about this?

Neither Horace nor his father feels that Camille has been unjustly treated. She has cursed the fatherland; that to them merits death. Horace senior, a fearsome patriot who wants to exercise his right to kill his son when he hears the false rumor that the latter has fled the field of combat, simply finds it wrong that a son of his should have been the one to kill Camille.

> Son crime, quoique énorme et digne du trépas,
> Était mieux impuni que puni par ton bras. [*]

And his son never apologizes for the murder, even to the judging king. Horace suggests indeed that he be executed for it, but only because it is unlikely that he will ever again repeat so glorious a feat as winning the duel and because lesser heroic acts in the future may tarnish his fame:

> La mort seule aujourd'hui peut conserver ma gloire. [†]

This surely is the ne plus ultra of *gloire*. And the king, who admits that those who have served the state so mightily are, at least temporarily, above the law, pardons the crime.

I think it is clear that Corneille was strongly of the opinion that the Roman Empire was a better thing for the world than a cosmos of warring nations, some of them barbaric, and that Roman Empires cannot be achieved without men such as Horace. On the other hand, he frankly faced the fact that such men are often endowed with brutal natures and that women such as Camille can expect little mercy at their hands. Horace represents the empire builder, Camille the empire victim. Both are true to life; each, at different times, is sympathetic and unsympathetic. Together they are Rome.

Perhaps it is Camille who has the last word in the curse that she flings at her native city. Her furious imprecations to her brother predict what happened a millennium later:

---

[*]However great her crime, however worthy of death, it had better gone unpunished than punished by you.

[†]Only death can now preserve my glory.

Rome, qui t'a vu naître et que ton cœur adore!
Rome, enfin que je hais parce qu'elle t'honore!
Puissent tous ces voisins ensemble conjurés
Saper ses fondements encore mal assurés!
Et si ce n'est assez de toute l'Italie
Que l'Orient contre elle à l'Occident s'allie;
Que cent peuples unis des bouts de l'univers
Passent pour la détruire et les monts et les mers!*

The parallel between the two Horaces, father and son, and Nazi Germany is obvious. One can see Corneille's men clearly enough in this passage from Iris Origo's *War in the Val D'Orcia* (1947) where she describes the retreating but not yet defeated German troops who, in 1944, had occupied her farm in Tuscany:

> As to the general morale, they are all quite frankly tired of the war and of five years away from their homes and families, appalled by the bombing of Germany, and depressed by the turn of events here and in France. But there is not one of them who does not still express his blind conviction that Germany *cannot* be beaten, and their equally blind belief in a terrible *Vergeltung* against England, which is close at hand. What form it will take, they say, they do not know, but the Führer has promised it to them, and he has never yet failed to keep his promise *to his own people*. Should this promise prove to have been only a bluff, then the whole nation's trust in the Führer would collapse. But, they hastily add, this will not, cannot happen.

---

*Rome, your birthplace and the adoration of your heart, Rome that I hate because she honors you, may her neighbors unite in undermining her yet unfinished foundations, and if all Italy is not enough for the task, may the east and west join forces against her, may a hundred nations from the ends of the world cross seas and mountains to destroy her!

Sophonisbe

The play *Sophonisbe* finds us well launched in the story of the Roman Empire. We have skipped from semi-legendary times, perhaps as early as the eighth century B.C., and are now in last stages of the Second Punic War. Hannibal, greatest of Carthaginian generals, has invaded northern Italy, crossing the Alps with his elephants (which we now know were a much smaller breed than the modern African pachyderm), and the senate in Rome has tried to induce Scipio Africanus, *their greatest general, to attack* Hannibal in Italy, but Scipio shrewdly prefers the much more successful ruse of moving his army to Africa and attacking Carthage directly, thus forcing Hannibal to rush home to defend his native city. This resulted in Scipio's triumph over Hannibal at Zama and Carthage's being brought to humiliating terms. The African metropolis, doomed by Cato's famous threat, had only fifty more years before its final and total destruction.

As the play involves Scipio's arrival in Africa from Sicily, we know that it is set in 204 B.C. The eponymous heroine is the passionately proud and flamingly patriotic daughter of the Carthaginian dictator Asdrubal and the consort of Syphax, king of Numidia, a nation wretchedly caught between the armies of Rome and Carthage and nervously teetering politically between the two. The tragedy is a study of Sophonisbe's desperate tactics in opposing in every way she can the ineluctable force of Roman aggrandisement, ending in her suicide to avoid being led, a captive

13

queen, in Scipio's triumph through the shouting streets of his world-conquering capital.

The two Roman officers who appear in the play, Lélius and Lépide, are shown as neither villains nor heroes. They are efficient agents of an occupying army, tough, courteous, and fair, carrying out their duties in a hard-boiled but, under the circumstances, reasonable manner. We are not concerned with their courage, honor, or *gloire*. Moral questions are the concern only of their defeated enemies and forced allies. But they are very much the concern of these.

Sophonisbe has much to say about her own *gloire,* but it is a *gloire* tempered—perhaps one might say coated—with vanity and even meanness. Is it possible that Corneille believed that such was the only kind of *gloire* available to women? Certainly Sophonisbe is very like the Roman princess of a later period of Roman history, Honoria, who appears in *Attila*. But like all of Corneille's heroines she seems real to us, even, or perhaps especially, when, as with many egotists, her brutal honesty verges on the comic. She puts her love of Carthage before her feelings for anyone else, lover, husband, all, and she insists on constantly flinging in their teeth just how *much* before it.

She has been originally betrothed to Massinisse, the former king of Numidia, with whom she has been and continues to be in love, but when his kingdom is overrun by a neighboring monarch, Syphax, Asdrubal requires his always obedient daughter to switch her affections and marry the elderly but doting new Numidian king and wean him from his Roman leanings. Sophonisbe complies, but when, as queen of Numidia, she finds that her husband is contemplating peace with his former allies, she fiercely insists that he break off negotiations and sends him forth to a battle which he knows he is doomed to lose. And even in demanding this sacrifice she doesn't hesitate to remind him that he owes her everything as she has given up her true love in order to tighten the ties between Numidia and Carthage.

> Moi, qui pour en étreindre à jamais les grands nœuds,
> Ai d'un amour si juste éteint les plus beaux feux!*

---

*I, who to forge forever the links between our nations, have quenched the fires of a true love!

14

The poor man, in obeying the command that will destroy him, offers only this faint but understandable complaint:

> Si vous m'aimiez, madame, il vous serait bien doux
> De voir comme je veux ne vous devoir qu'à vous:
> Vous ne vous plairiez pas à montrer dans votre âme
> Les restes odieux d'une première flamme.[*]

And when Syphax and his army are captured by the Romans, Sophonisbe does not hesitate to repudiate her marriage and give her hand to her old lover Massinisse, who, it is true, is now an ally of Rome, but whom she loves, who has been renamed king of Numidia and whose influence with Scipio may save her from sharing the fate of Syphax and being shamefully exhibited in a triumph. Of course, she is willing to die to avoid this.

But even in the temporary elation of being reunited with her lover, she wants to be sure that Massinisse knows just where she stands in all this. In everything she has done, as in everything that she will do, Carthage comes first and foremost:

> Quand j'épousai Syphax, je n'y fus point forcée;
> De quelques traits pour vous que l'amour m'eût blessée,
> Je vous quittai sans peine, et tous mes vœux trahis
> Cédèrent avec joie au bien de mon pays.
> En un mot, j'ai reçu du ciel pour mon partage
> L'aversion de Rome et l'amour de Carthage.[†]

Indeed, her patriotism seems to be what the play is all about; Corneille contrasts the fiery and noble spirit of the dauntless opponent of Rome with the glacier-like inevitability of the Latin conquest of the world. Is he telling us what wonderful things may have been sacrificed to the civilizing yet smothering advance of the empire he so admired? It seems so, for he never ceased to be a relentless realist. But at the same time he does not allow himself to wax too sentimental about his heroine. She too has her flaws.

---

[*]If you really loved me, madam, it would gratify you to recognize that I'd rather owe you to none but yourself; you wouldn't take such pleasure in showing off the unsightly remnants of your earlier flame.

[†]I was not forced to marry Syphax, and although I loved you I left you without pain, happy to break my vows in the service of my country. In a word, my destiny from heaven has been to hate Rome and love Carthage.

It is not entirely clear, for example, that when Sophonisbe sends Syphax out to his defeat she is motivated wholly by her apprehension that a negotiated peace will not be in the best interests of Carthage. There is also the factor that such a peace will bring about the marriage, already arranged by the Romans, between their ally Massinisse and Éryxe, queen of the Getuliens, now a captive and slave of Sophonisbe. Rome plans to restore Éryxe to the kingdom which Syphax and Sophonisbe have taken from her and link her to their cause.

Sophonisbe's confidant, Herminie, to whom she confesses her dread of this result, points out that her mistress is capricious. Why should she resent handing over the captive queen to the man she has rejected in favor of Syphax? Because, as Sophonisbe frankly admits, one never wishes a rejected lover to console himself.

> Qui rejette un beau feu n'aime pas que l'on l'éteigne:
> On se plaît à régner sur ce que l'on dédaigne.*

And when, after the defeat of Syphax, Massinisse, still amorous of the proud queen who spurned him, refuses the bride offered him by the Romans and offers his hand and new crown to the now captive Sophonisbe, she exultantly tells her confidant that beating Éryxe to the draw is the greatest joy of all.

> Et c'est, pour peu qu'on aime, une extrême douceur
> De pouvoir accorder sa gloire avec son cœur:
> Mais c'en est une ici bien autre, et sans égale,
> D'enlever, et si tôt, ce prince à ma rivale.†

Herminie carries this enthusiasm even further. She regrets that Éryxe's self-control is such that she does not manifest her chagrin!

> Je voudrais qu'elle vit un peu plus son malheur,
> Qu'elle en fit hautement éclater la douleur.‡

---

*Rejecting a man's love needn't mean that one wishes to see it extinguished; it is pleasing to rule over a lover disdained.

†It is sweet when one's glory and love are in accord, but it is sweeter yet to snatch the prince so quickly from my rival.

‡I only wish that she had a clearer view of her misfortune and that her wailing were more audible.

Surely the meanest words ever spoken by a confidant in classic tragedy!

But when all turns black for the heroine, when Masinisse proves unable to persuade Scipio to recognize his marriage to her or even to release her from the humiliation of being a part of the Roman general's triumph, she rises above pettiness to magnificence. When Massinisse sends her a bottle of poison as the only way for her to escape this shame, she scorns him for not taking it himself.

> Plus esclave en son camp que je suis ici,
> Il devait de son sort prendre même souci.
> Quel présent nuptial d'un époux à sa femme!*

She summons Éryxe before taking the lethal dose and proudly offers her back her now devalued lover:

> Je l'ai pris magnanime, et vous le rends perfide;
> Je vous le rends sans cœur, et l'ai pris intrépide;
> Je l'ai pris le plus grand des princes africains,
> Et le rends, pour tout dire, esclave des Romains.†

But even Éryxe doesn't want him now. After Sophonisbe's suicide, she explains to the Roman Lélius that she will accept her nation back and govern it under Roman sway, for such a subsidiary position is less shameful for a woman than for a man. But she will not wed Massinisse or share a crown with him.

> Je suis femme et mon sexe accablé d'impuissance
> Ne reçoit pas d'affront par cette dépendance;
> Mais je n'aurai jamais à rougir d'un époux
> Qu'on voie ainsi que moi ne régner que sous vous.‡

---

*More a slave in his camp than I am here, he should look to his own fate. What a wedding gift to send to a wife!

†I took him from you generous and return him a traitor; I send him back heartless, though I had him brave; I was proud to possess the greatest of African princes, but I scorn to keep the slave of Rome.

‡I am a woman, and the weaker sex is not insulted by such dependence, but I would never tolerate a husband who suffered it.

17

Corneille, however, is not through with her yet. The final words of the play are given to Lélius. He says, with a presumably cynical shrug, "laissons-en faire au temps."[*] As in *Le Cid*, where the audience is allowed to suspect that Chimène will relent and ultimately wed the hero, the viewers of *Sophonisbe* are left with the suggestion that the all-powerful Romans will get their way in the end. And what does this say for the *gloire* of their enemies, reduced to the frankly collaborating Massinisse and the already compromising Éryxe?

---

[*]Time will tell.

Nicomède

T he action of the play occurs in 183 B.C., for we learn of the
  death of Hannibal, who, having escaped the pursuing Roman
legions to what he believed was the safety of the court of
King Prusias of Bithynia, has taken poison on learning that his
treacherous host was planning to turn him over to his enemy. Asia
Minor was still independent of Rome, but Prusias, cowering
before what he apprehended to be the wave of the future, had
deemed it expedient to come to terms, however basely, with an
ineluctable force.

So far, Corneille follows history. But he soon embroiders on
it. Arsinoé, the unscrupulous and dominating second wife of
Prusias, hopes to persuade her weak spouse not only to leave his
kingdom to their Roman-educated son, Attale, at the expense of
Nicomède, the son and heir of the king's first marriage, but also
to give Attale as a bride his half brother's betrothed, the young
Laodice, queen of Armenia, who lives in Prusias's court as his
ward and dependent. Nicomède, however, is the hero of the
people and the brilliant general whose military genius has added
Cappadocia, Pontus, and Galatia to his father's rule. Also, he is in
love with Laodice and she with him. Arsinoé will need all her
guile to execute her plan. But she has much of it to use.

She lures Nicomède by trickery away from his army so that he
finds himself alone and virtually defenseless in the hostile court of
his father and faced with his direst foe, Flaminius, the Roman

19

ambassador. The action of the play consists of the hero's maneuvers in turning his highly vulnerable situation into a winning one. He accomplishes this largely by the simple force of his character and the scathing intelligence of his wit. At all times he dominates the scene, flinging searing home truths at his treacherous father and feline stepmother, defying and brilliantly insulting the Roman ambassador and sarcastically excoriating his presumptuous half brother. One is never put off by his exuberant pride in his own glory, first, because it is justified by the facts and, second, because he is at all times in the very grip of his foes. He is the most winning and attractive of all of Corneille's heroes, including the Cid.

Of course, he prevails in the end; it would be too odious if he didn't. The local population rises to deliver him, and his half brother, at the last minute, comes over to his side. The play is really more what was called a heroic comedy than it is a tragedy. Such a comedy didn't have to be funny; it could be a serious drama where only a few bad guys got killed.

What is of particular interest to us is what the play tells us of Corneille's attitude toward the Roman Empire. At this point Rome has defeated Carthage; the Mediterranean has become a Latin sea. But what has happened to *gloire?* Is it part of the irresistible military advance over the borders of smaller nations that topple before it? Is it part of putting pressure on a weak Bithynian monarch to make him hand over a gallant Carthaginian general to be exhibited in a humiliating triumph? Is it making and unmaking marriages and crowns among puppet rulers?

Flaminius, who makes little secret of his determination to direct the policies of the Bithynian government under the shallow guise of diplomatic talks, is cool, clever, dispassionate, and courteous—at least until it becomes necessary for him to shed the velvet glove. He is serenely confident in the glorious destiny of his people. No one in his day, he states flatly, can rule a kingdom without the support of Rome. He warns the young queen of Armenia:

> Songez mieux ce qu'est Rome, et ce qu'elle peut faire;
> Et si vous vous aimez, craignez de lui déplaire.

Carthage étant détruite, Antiochus défait,
Rien de nos volontés ne peut troubler l'effet.
Tout fléchit sur la terre, et tout tremble sur l'onde;
Et Rome est aujourd'hui la maîtresse du monde.*

Even Nicomède concedes that Flaminius is only doing his duty as a Roman when he seeds dissension among nations not yet conquered:

Non que je veuille à Rome imputer quelque crime.
Du grand art de régner elle suit la maxime;
Et son ambassadeur ne fait que son devoir,
Quand il veut entre nous partager le pouvoir.†

Flaminius is at his most Roman when he instructs Attale that his courtship of the queen of Armenia has been countenanced only so long as Attale himself was not the heir to a crown, but that with the change in his prospects he must give her up. Attale, protesting, is treated like a naughty boy.

Pour ne vous faire pas de réponse trop rude
Sur ce beau coup d'essai de votre ingratitude,
Suivez votre caprice, offensez vos amis,
Vous êtes souverain, et tout vous est permis.
Mais puisqu'enfin ce jour vous doit faire connaître
Que Rome vous a fait ce que vous allez être,
Que perdant son appui vous ne ferez plus rien,
Que le roi vous l'a dit, souvenez-vous-en bien.‡

---

*Learn better what Rome is and what Rome can do, and if you know what's best for you, fear to displease her. With Carthage destroyed and Antiochus defeated, the earth bows to us and the sea trembles. Rome is mistress of the world.

†Not that I wish to impute a crime to Rome. She is simply practicing the great art of reigning, and her ambassador is only doing his duty in setting us against each other.

‡Not to make too rude a reply to your fine expression of ingratitude, let me simply put it this way: follow up with your fancy and irritate your friends; you're the king; all is permitted. But since you're bound at last to find out that Rome has made you whatever you may become, and that without her support you can do nothing, it would be wise to remember what the king told you.

Attale's change of attitude from that of the spoiled brat who aspires, with the backing of Rome, to the hand of his big brother's fiancée, to that of admirer and ultimate rescuer of the same brother is the most interesting development in the play. Voltaire thought that Corneille spoiled this development by having it motivated not by the emergence of Attale's better nature but simply by his disillusionment with Rome's willingness to procure his bride for him.

It is time to say a word about Voltaire and Corneille. The former in 1765 edited a twelve-volume edition of the latter's work with copious comments and footnotes. Despite his intense admiration for a very few verses in each play, Voltaire tended to find the tragedian lacking in high seriousness and his characters more often vulgarly comic than noble. It is something of a mystery why so great a mind should have been so long preoccupied with material it did not relish. But it is clear to me that Voltaire utterly failed to appreciate the persistent realism that is the dominant characteristic of Corneille's poetry. If this quality puts you off, as it did Voltaire, if it makes his characters seem eccentric, grotesque, or simply silly, his plays are not for you. But to me it makes total sense that a young man, spoiled rotten by Roman masters who seek to make a weakling and a puppet of him, would be much more apt to turn against them when they cease to give him what he wants than because he suddenly appreciates his brother's superior virtues. That Attale becomes a man only when he discovers what the Romans are really up to is perfectly logical to me.

It would appear, anyway, that *gloire* has passed from the conquering Roman legions to the brave souls who still resist them, of whom Nicomède, of course, is the shining symbol. But what is to become of Nicomède if he is not to succumb to Rome? Presumably he can forestall their victory for a few decades, but can he do it in any other way than conquering nations which Rome might otherwise have conquered and banding them together into an equally powerful empire? Nicomède himself seems highly enthusiastic about such a plan. He boasts that he will extend the rule of Bithynia to the banks of the Hellespont and to the furthest shores of the Aegean; he even emulates Alexander in claiming that all of Asia is open to his ambition.

So what is the essential difference between the Rome of the cool and cynical Flaminius who hounds the brave Hannibal to his death and the Bithynia of the noble Nicomède who gazes east for new worlds to conquer? Is it simply a question of chronology? That the fresher, younger nation has more dash and charm than the older, established one? At least while it is fresher and younger? Perhaps. Nicomède is a kind of Horace with the brutality rubbed out; he is the ultimate hero. And is it the fate of heroes to make endless wars? Until one of them develops a weapon so lethal that it will destroy the world or scare it into a snarling peace? *Gloire*, in the last analysis, is gore. Corneille, the eternal realist, can face it. Is it possible that he can even like it?

He might at this point object. He may have seen a solution to the problem of war in the ultimate domination of one absolute monarchy. He had no use for democracy, even for the limited public rule of the Roman republic; he may have seen the cause of Latin decline in this and in the inability of the empire to establish a viable system of succession. But there seems to have been little limit to his admiration of Louis XIV. It was probably the Sun King who personified *gloire* for him. The "grand monarque" may have been his answer to everything.

Sertorius

The year is 72 B.C.; the empire is in disarray. Sulla in the capital has seized the supreme power and established a bloody dictatorship, suppressing the ancient rights and privileges of Roman citizens. The once noble city has become a moral cesspool; honor and virtue are held in ridicule. But the old and illustrious general Sertorius has set up a base for the opposition in Aragon where he has assembled a rival senate of refugee legislators and united the many tribes of the Iberian Peninsula under his standard. He has pledged himself to reunite the empire under libertarian principles. As the play opens Sulla has sent his new son-in-law and proposed successor, Pompey, to Aragon under a flag of truce to seek a negotiated peace.

Corneille, unfortunately, spoils this dramatic setting by cluttering his stage with cryptic situations and unsympathetic characters, which all the nobility of some of his finest verses cannot redeem. That the play was one of his most popular when performed in 1662 seems strange to a modern reader. Consider some of the twists in the plot. Sulla—or Sylla, as Corneille would have it—has induced the ambitious Pompée to divorce the wife he loves, Aristie, to wed the dictator's daughter. Aristie had fled to join Sertorius whom she is willing to marry, though lovelessly, in order to link her forces more closely to his in the war against Rome. But she warns him that she still loves her unfaithful spouse and will return to him if he repudiates his new wife. Viriate, queen of

25

Lusitania, wishes, also lovelessly, to wed the aging Sertorius for the same reason as Aristie. Perpenna, Sertorius's treacherous lieutenant, is in love (unconvincingly) with Viriate and plans secretly to murder his chief if the latter cannot induce the proud queen to marry him. And where is the unhappy general in all of this? He dares not marry either Aristie or Viriate. Should he wed the former her unreasonably jealous ex-husband will break the truce, and if he rejects the queen she will pull out her valuable troops. And he further infuriates the dangerous Perpenna by offering *him* to the queen and subjecting the lieutenant to her scornful refusal. To make matters even worse he is secretly in love, in mournful hopelessness, with Viriate himself.

The general mix-up comes perilously close to comedy. The two haughty ladies are almost ludicrous in their boasts that love with them will always lag behind the leading thrust of duty. Hear Viriate:

Ce ne sont pas les sens que mon amour consulte:
Il hait des passions l'impétueux tumulte;
Et son feu, que j'attache aux soins de ma grandeur,
Dédaigne tout mélange avec leur folle ardeur.*

And now Aristie:

Laissons, Seigneur, laissons pour les petites âmes
Ce commerce rampant de soupirs et de flammes;
Et ne nous unissons que pour mieux soutenir
La liberté que Rome est prête à voir finir.†

And what are we meant to think of Pompée, who wishes to cling to his cake of domestic love while consuming it in the interests of his ambition? In a ridiculous scene he urges Aristie to give up her plan of marrying Sertorius and wait for the death of

---

*My love never consults the senses. It despises the chaos of passion. Its pure fire, guardian of my greatness, disdains any connection with the madness of desire.

†Oh, sir, let us leave to petty souls the sordid business of sighs and flames, and seek only in our union a way to salvage the civil liberties which Rome is ready to extinguish.

the aging Sylla when he can repudiate the tyrant's daughter and take back his true love in a Rome redeemed from dictatorship. Aristie rejects this, but she still holds the door open a crack:

> Non que je puisse aimer aucun autre que vous;
> Mais pour venger ma gloire il me faut un époux:
> Il m'en faut un illustre, et dont la renommée. . .*

Yet what are the awkward traits of these characters but evidence of what I have in an earlier essay described as Corneille's wholesome and interesting realism? Are there not women who will prefer power and glory to love and who will freely marry to promote themselves or a cause? And who will even boast about it? Have we not all known Pompées who will divorce and remarry for advantage and still try to hang on to earlier loves? And not even be ashamed of it? Yes, of course. But in drama they must be shown up or at least contrasted with characters more sympathetic. There are none here. And in the end they all get what they want except Perpenna, who has murdered the hero and must himself be punished by a hundred stabs.

Sertorius is probably glad enough to die. His is hardly a tragedy. He has fumbled everything. He does not know where to turn, and in the end he is simply stalling for time. He sadly learns that his beloved Viriate has no share in his zeal to bring a decent government to Rome. Hers is a peculiar pride, one that would not be found outside the world of Corneille. The real world? She says that true joy consists in having things that other people *don't* have; it is the bliss of felt advantage.

> La liberté n'est rien quand tout le monde est libre;
> Mais il est beau de l'être, et voir tout l'univers
> Soupirer sous le joug et gémir dans les fers;
> Il est beau d'étaler cette prérogative
> Aux yeux du Rhône esclave et de Rome captive.†

---

*Not that I can love anyone but you, yet I must have a husband to avenge my glory, and an illustrious and famous one . . .

†Liberty is nothing when all the world is free. What is really fine is to enjoy it when the rest of the world is groaning in chains, to dangle one's freedom in the eyes of Roman captives and slaves.

Corneille ends his tragedy by resorting to the Greek god from the machine. Once Sertorius has been assassinated by Perpenna's men, a messenger arrives from Rome to announce that Sylla has resigned and that his daughter is dead. Pompée can now assume the executive power, restore liberty, remarry Aristie, and reunite the empire. Even Viriate is content to recognize the suzerainty of Rome, though, like Éryxe in *Sophonisbe,* she must make it clear that she will never marry, as it cannot be fit for a *man* to wear a crown subject to another.

The best scene in the play and the one for which it is most remembered is that between Sertorius and Pompée in which the latter tries unsuccessfully to persuade the former to give up the war and make his peace with Sylla. Corneille's contemporary audiences apparently had an inexhaustible appetite for this sort of political give and take. And this scene is certainly interesting, covering as it does different aspects of dealing with threatened civil liberties, as relevant to our century as to his.

Pompée starts with the argument that it is better to work behind the scenes of dictatorial rule, waiting for better times, than to wade in seas of blood. He says of Sylla:

> Je lui prête mon bras sans engager mon âme;
> Je m'abandonne au cours de sa félicité,
> Tandis que tous mes vœux sont pour la liberté;
> Et c'est ce qui me force à garder une place
> Qu'usurperaient sans moi l'injustice et l'audace,
> Afin que, Sylla mort, ce dangereux pouvoir
> Ne tombe qu'en des mains qui sachent leur devoir.[*]

Sertorius replies that people are saying that Pompée is really only out for himself:

> Mais si je m'en rapporte aux esprits soupçonneux,
> Vous aidez aux Romains à faire essai d'un maître,

---

[*]I loan him my arm without committing my soul. I abandon myself to the tide of his good fortune while praying for the return of our liberties. I make a point of safeguarding a place that would otherwise be seized by injustice and audacity, so that, Sylla once dead, the supreme power will fall only in hands that know how to use it.

Sous ce flatteur espoir qu'un jour vous pourrez l'être.
La main qui les opprime, et que vous soutenez,
Les accoutume au joug que vous leur destinez.*

Pompée hits back with the suggestion that Sertorius's rule in Iberia is really an equal dictatorship.

Les titres différents ne font rien à la chose;†
Vous imposez des lois ainsi qu'il en impose.

And when Sertorius answers that he runs an open place of exile, ruling more by love than by fear, Pompée retorts:

Et votre empire est d'autant plus dangereux,
Qu'il rend de vos vertus les peuples amoureux,
Qu'en assujettissant vous avez l'art de plaire,
Qu'on croit n'être en vos fers qu'esclave volontaire,
Et que la liberté trouvera peu de jour
A détruire un pouvoir que fait régner l'amour.‡

That might have been the argument used by labor leaders against non-union "benevolent dictatorships." As Corneille ends the play with the triumph of Pompée and the revealed impotence (perhaps in every sense) of the old general who can only assert his wish to die when Viriate, seeking to uncover his love, pretends a willingness to accept Perpenna, one wonders if the playwright believed that Pompée's was the better way of handling a hated dictatorship. Perhaps, in view of the rapid turnover of governments in Rome, waiting was indeed the wiser policy. But in our own day we have sadly learned that a Hitler or a Stalin or a Mussolini, having once gained total control of the military and the media, is virtually impregnable.

---

*But if I listen to certain suspicious folk, you are teaching the Romans to make trial of a master in the hope of one day being yourself that. The hand that oppresses them, and which you support, is accustoming them to the yoke that you hope to continue.

†A different name needn't change the meaning. Your laws are his laws.

‡And your rule is all the more dangerous in that it makes the people enamored of your virtues. You have the art of so pleasing your subjects that they deem themselves voluntary slaves who would have little to gain in upsetting a leader who governs through love.

Mithridate

The year 1673 marked the admission to the French Academy of Jean Racine, Corneille's younger rival in the theatre, and the production of Racine's *Mithridate,* much admired by the court, as it would have been, even without its great merit, as a favorite play of the king's. It is certainly the most "Louis XIV" of Racine's tragedies and the only one in which he seems to challenge the older playwright on his home territory: that of heroic and patriotic drama. The critical arguments as to which of the two was the greater playwright have usually played up their differences in subject matter and treatment. As Edmond Pilon and René Groos state in the preface to their 1931 edition of Racine: "Le reproche le plus constant qu'il essaya, et qui le poursuivit au moins jusqu'à *Phèdre,* ce fut d'avoir substitué à l'héroïsme des personnages de Corneille un réalisme qui paraissait grossier. On jugeait Pyrrhus trop violent, Andromaque trop éprise, Néron trop cruel, Titus plus désesperé qu'il ne se doit, Phèdre plus 'effrontée' qu'il n'est supportable. Corneille lui-même se plaignait qu'il peignît nos faiblesses. En le miracle de Racine, la vertu suprême de cette peinture de passions, c'est peut-être aussi son incomparable et saisissante variété. Toutes les formes de l'amour, jusqu'aux plus exquises, jusqu'aux plus furieuses, toutes les formes de l'ambition, jusqu'aux plus criminelles, tour à tour et tout à la fois les visages les plus purs et les plus atroces; tous les feux du paganisme

31

et toutes les pudeurs chrétiennes, les tragédies du cœur et celle de la politique. . . ."*

I think it quite possible that in *Mithridate* Racine was expanding his variety to demonstrate that he could beat Corneille at his own game. The play closely resembles Corneille's *Nicomède*. We are again in the Middle East, in 63 B.C. in Cimmerian Bosporus on the Black Sea, where the forces of the veteran warrior Mithridate, king of Pontus, are seeking to rally and recover themselves from a seemingly desperate defeat by the Romans. Mithridate is rumored to be dead, but this is only a ploy to cover his retreat, typical of the wily old monarch who has for forty years provided the major opposition to the Roman conquest of the world. His two sons, the hero, Xipharès, and the villainous secret ally of Rome, Pharnace, not knowing that their father's death is a ruse, clash over their joint love of the beautiful Monime, the unwilling betrothed of Mithridate, now supposedly released from her vows. She, of course, like a proper heroine, loves the gallant and brave Xipharès, who has adored her in silence before her forced engagement to the old warrior and who despises his sneaky brother. The sudden return of Mithridate provides the action of the play.

He is a patriot as furious and violent as the elder Horace, a magnificent figure of military might and dauntless ambition, who thunders defiance at his Roman enemies, and plots, even in defeat, to lead his troops, like Hannibal, across Europe and down the Italian peninsula in an ally-gathering march to sack Rome itself while its legions are engaged in Asia Minor. *Gloire,* as in *Nicomède,* has passed from the Latins to their eastern opponents, and Mithridate incarnates this virtue.

But there is a signal difference between Mithridate and a

---

*The most constant reproach to his work is to have substituted for the heroism of Corneille's protagonists a realism too crude. Critics have found Pyrrhus too violent, Andromaque too dedicated, Nero too cruel, Titus too despairing, Phedre too bold. Corneille himself complained that Racine painted our weaknesses. But the miracle of Racine, the supreme virtue of this painter of the human passions, is his wonderful variety. All forms of love, the most exquisite and the most furious; all forms of ambition, the noblest and the most criminal; the furies of paganism and the restraints of Christianity; the tragedies of the heart and those of politics [are to be found in his theatre].

Corneille hero. The former is unscrupulous, tricky, jealous, vindictive and cruel. He has slaughtered as many as a hundred thousand prisoners of war at one time. And we learn that he has already put two other sons to death for slight cause and will not hesitate to kill any of his mistresses who has caused him the least jealousy. Suspicious that Monime, whom he has first tried to seduce but whom he has at last agreed to marry to satisfy his senile craving, may be harboring a secret love for Xipharès, he tricks her into a confession by craftily telling her that he is too old for her and has decided to wed her to this favorite son. Furious at finding that the young couple are indeed united by a mutual passion, although they regard themselves as duty bound to respect Monime's engagement, he resolves to kill them both and is only prevented by an assault on his castle by the Romans, alerted to his proposed raid on their capitol by the treacherous Pharnace. The Roman onslaught is finally repulsed by Xipharès, but Mithridate, believing all lost, has stabbed himself to avoid capture. Victory induces repentance, and he conveys his dying blessing on Xipharès and Monime.

The figure of Mithridate is grander and greater than any in all of Corneille, and the language in which he expresses his megalomania is as fine as any in *Horace* or *Le Cid*. When the king suspects, quite rightly, that Monime has agreed to marry him only in obedience to her parents, he lashes out at her magnificently, instructing her that at the lowest point of his fortunes she should still be honored to be his bride:

> Mes malheurs, en un mot, me font-ils mépriser?
> Ah, pour tenter encore de nouvelles conquêtes,
> Quand je ne verrais pas de routes toutes prêtes,
> Quand le sort ennemi m'aurait jeté plus bas,
> Vaincu, persécuté, sans secours, sans États,
> Errant de mers en mers, et moins roi que pirate,
> Conservant pour tous biens, le nom de Mithridate,
> Apprenez que, suivi d'un nom si glorieux,
> Partout de l'univers j'attacherais les yeux,
> Et qu'il n'est pas de rois, s'ils sont dignes de l'être,

Qui, sur le trône assis, n'enviassent peut-être
Au-dessus de leur gloire un naufrage élevé,
Que Rome, et quarante ans, ont à peine achevé.[*]

And hear him outlining to his sons his plan to seize Rome:

Annibal l'a prédit, croyons-en ce grand homme,
Jamais on ne vaincra les Romains que dans Rome.
Noyons-la dans son sang justement répandu.
Brûlons ce Capitole où j'étais attendu.
Détruisons ses honneurs, et faisons disparaître
La honte de cent rois, et la mienne peut-être.[†]

And his dying words are best of all:

Mais au moins quelque joie en mourant me console:
J'expire environné d'ennemis que j'immole;
Dans leur sang odieux j'ai pu tremper mes mains,
Et mes derniers regards ont vu fuir les Romains.[‡]

If Racine, as Corneille averred, is painting our weaknesses, the savage side of the old hero makes him come alive as no other character in French classic tragedy does. Perhaps his being so much in love with Monime seems a little out of character. One might have inferred simply lust from such a world ravager, but Racine makes it clear that it is more than that. Mithridate's first address to his betrothed on his return is positively gallant:

---

[*]Have my misfortunes caused me to be despised? Even supposing that I should no longer see ways available for new conquests, that a cruel fate should cast me even further down, that wandering from sea to sea, less king than pirate, with no asset but the name of Mithridates: know well, madam, that, armed with that alone, I should still attract the eyes of the universe, and that there exists no sovereign worthy of the title who, however firmly seated on his throne, would not envy a shipwrecked hero whose glory Rome in forty years has not achieved.

[†]Hannibal predicted it; let us believe that great man. Rome can only be conquered in Rome. Let us drown her in her own blood and burn the capitol. Let us avenge the shame of a hundred kings—and maybe even my own.

[‡]But I have at least this joy in dying: I expire on the pile of enemies I have slaughtered. I can dip my hands in their hated blood. My final vision is that of fleeing foes.

Madame, enfin le ciel près de vous me rappelle,
Et secondant du moins mes plus tendres souhaits
Vous rend à mon amour plus belle que jamais.[*]

He will treat her roughly enough when his jealousy is aroused, but in the meantime he shows a Gallic elegance in his manners. Perhaps theatregoers in the Paris of Corneille and Racine found elderly lovers, at least among males, sympathetic; there are certainly several such in Corneille's drama: *vide* the eponymous hero Sertorius and Martian in *Pulchérie*. But Racine is careful to contrast the old man's possessive and tyrannical affection with the son's more discreet but equally strong passion for the same object. Xipharès, noble in mind, brave in war, and true in love, can nonetheless control his feelings so as to make the dismal doom of his beloved in being wed to an old man against her will as painless as possible. There is no hint on his part of lack of feeling; his love for her is such that her distress is more to him than his own. Xipharès and Monime are the most attractive lovers in Racine's theatre, and the only ones to be united at the final curtain, unless you count Iphigénie and Achille, whose happiness at the end of *Iphigénie* is clouded by a war in which we know the hero will be killed.

If Racine was in conscious competition with Corneille in writing *Mithridate,* he must have been pleased at his success. The play was an immediate hit. Madame de Sévigné wrote to her daughter, Madame de Grignan: "*Mithridate* est une pièce charmante. On y pleure; on y est dans une continuelle admiration, on la voit trente fois, on la trouve plus belle la trentième que la première."[†]

---

[*]Madam, at last the heavens send me back to you, and, answering my tenderest wishes, they have rendered you lovelier than ever.

[†]*Mithridate* is a charming play. It makes one cry; it never ceases to amaze; you see it thirty times, and it's just as beautiful the thirtieth time as the first.

La Mort de Pompée

Here at last we meet Julius Caesar, the greatest Roman of them all, in 48 B.C., just four years before his assassination in the senate at the foot of the statue, "which all the while ran blood," of the man whose death provides the title for the play. A long struggle for control of the empire has finally narrowed down to that between Caesar and Pompey. The latter may have been the hero who cleansed the seas of piracy and defeated the indomitable Mithridates, but his luck has run out, and he has just lost his last battle at Pharsala in Greece and fled with his wife, Cornelia, to asylum in Egypt, hotly pursued by the navy of his now all-powerful rival.

Corneille was able to surmount the seeming restrictions of the classic couplet in his vivid and ghastly evocation of the terrible aftermath of the battle.

> Ses fleuves teints de sang et rendus plus rapides
> Par le débordement de tant de parricides,
> Cet horrible débris d'aigles, d'armes, de chars,
> Sur les champs empestés confusément épars,
> Ces montagnes de morts privés d'honneurs suprêmes,
> Que la nature force à se venger eux-mêmes,
> Et dont les troncs pourris exhalent dans les vents
> De quoi faire la guerre au reste des vivants,

Sont les titres affreux dont le droit de l'épée,
Justifiant César, a condamné Pompée.[*]

The young Ptolemy, or Ptolemée, however, though he owes
his kingdom to Pompée, nonetheless heeds the advice of wicked
counselors and has his former savior murdered and his head
handed to the now-arriving César. Cléopâtre, Ptolemée's sister,
whose half of the kingdom he has usurped and who remains his
captive, is outraged and takes her complaint to César, who falls
under her spell and is delighted to have the wicked counselors put
to death. Ptolemée retaliates with an attempted palace coup
against the Romans in the suppression of which he loses his life,
leaving the throne for his sister. A subplot is provided by Pompée's
revengeful widow, Cornélie, who defies her generous capturer and
boldly tells César that when she receives her promised release she
will continue a war to the death with him. She scorns the tool of
assassination, however, and actually warns him of a conspiracy
against his life. When the curtain falls on a triumphant César,
who now plans to divorce Calpurnie and wed Cléopâtre despite
Rome's well-known prejudice against queens, Cornélie darkly
predicts what everyone in the audience knows will happen:

Je sais quelle est ta flamme et quelles sont ses forces,
Que tu n'ignores pas comme on fait les divorces,
Que ton amour t'aveugle, et que pour l'épouser
Rome n'a point de lois que tu n'oses briser;
Mais sache aussi qu'alors la jeunesse romaine
Se croira tout permis sur l'époux d'une reine,
Et que de cet hymen tes amis indignés
Vengeront sur ton sang leurs avis dédaignés.[†]

---

[*]The rivers reddened with blood whose currents are even accelerated by the
immersion of so many corpses, the plains covered with a hideous debris of
eagles, arms, and chariots, the piles of dead deprived of funeral honors, which
nature forces to avenge themselves by exhaling fumes fatal to the living—such is
the plight to which the fortunes of war, favoring Caesar, have condemned the
army of Pompey.

[†]I am quite aware of your love and how strong it is, and that you think,
blinded by passion, that you know all about divorce and that there is no law you
dare not break to obtain one, but you may learn that the youth of Rome will

All of this adds up more to a historical fresco than to a tragedy. The story teems with gruesome events: the battle in Greece, the murder of Pompée, the recovery of his body flung in the sea, the vengeance wrought by César, the attempt on César's life, the suicide of Ptolemée—yet all must take place off stage. We learn what is happening through a series of gasping messengers just back from the carnage. Voltaire for once put his finger on just what was wrong and right in this play: "Mais *Pompée* n'est point une véritable tragédie; c'est une tentative que fait Corneille pour mettre sur la scène des morceaux excellents, qui ne faisaient point un tout; c'est un ouvrage d'un genre unique, qu'il ne faudrait pas imiter, et que son génie, animé par la grandeur romaine, pouvait seul faire réussir. Trente beaux vers de Corneille valent beaucoup mieux qu'une pièce mediocre."[*]

The characters lack substance. Nothing could be more different from Shakespeare's beguiling Egyptian queen that the prim and virtuous Cléopâtre who responds to Charmion's remark that love appears to have scant power over the queen's will:

> Les princes ont cela de leur haute naissance;
> Leur âme dans leur sang prend des impressions
> Qui dessous leur vertu rangent leurs passions;
> Leur générosité soumet tout à leur gloire;
> Tout est illustre en eux quand ils daignent se croire.[†]

She may have a kind of love for César, but it's the lord of the world she wishes to marry. And César's love for her, despite all of what Voltaire calls their "ridiculous" and lengthy exchange of gallantries, cannot be much more than an older man's lust for a

---

consider anything permissible in dealing with the husband of a queen and may avenge with your blood their outraged beliefs.

[*]*Pompée* isn't a real tragedy at all: it's a device by which Corneille managed to put on the stage some excellent parts which fail to add up to a whole. It's a unique production and should never be imitated; it took all of his genius, animated by his admiration for the grandeur of Rome, to pull it off. Thirty of his beautiful couplets make even a mediocre play worthwhile.

[†]Princes owe that to their exalted birth. Their soul receives a rule with their blood which makes their passions subject to their virtue. All is secondary to their glory; all goes right with them if they will only believe in themselves.

pretty young thing. We simply don't believe him—and wonder if Corneille meant us to—when César tells her that during the battle of Pharsala he was thinking more of the right to win her hand as a conqueror than he was of subduing Pompée. The possible cynical side of César is brought out by Achorée who has watched him closely when Ptolemée offered him Pompée's severed head. Wasn't his disgust and anger at such an act of treachery to a former benefactor put on for the benefit of posterity? Wasn't he playing the great man's generous attitude to a beaten foe in punishing his assassins? And didn't his heart secretly exult at this rapid disposition of an opponent troublesome even in defeat? Achorée thinks so.

> Et je dirai, si j'ose en faire conjecture,
> Que par un mouvement commun à la nature,
> Quelque maligne joie en son cœur s'élevait,
> Dont sa gloire indignée à peine le sauvait. *

Common to nature! That is again and again what gives their peculiar distinction to Corneille's heroes. Just when we wonder if they are not too noble to be quite believable, he will jolt us with some mean detail of their only too credible human weakness. We shall see that Napoleon favored the actor in *Cinna* who interpreted Augustus's noble forgiveness of the conspirators who had plotted to kill him as a public relations gesture. But in Pompée we need some character to attract our sympathy; history alone is a bit too cold for the stage.

Cornélie is supposed by many to save the play. Yet she is certainly a bore with her obsessional desire for personal vengeance and her ineluctable faith in the absolute virtuousness of her credo. Is she meant to be the ultimate example of the *gloire* that Corneille so admired the Romans for cultivating? Or should we see her as a noble but misguided fanatic? Her language, anyway, is admirable. Here is her farewell to César:

---

*And I dare to conjecture that, in common with other human beings, his heart glowed with a secret and malicious joy of which his better nature was hardly aware.

Mais ne présume pas toucher par là mon cœur.
La perte que j'ai faite est trop irréparable;
La source de ma haine est trop inépuisable;
A l'égal de mes jours je la ferai durer;
Je veux vivre avec elle, avec elle expirer.
Je t'avouerai, pourtant, comme vraiment Romaine,
Que pour toi mon estime est égale à ma haine;
Que l'une et l'autre est juste, et montre le pouvoir,
L'une de ta vertu, l'autre de mon devoir.[*]

Did Corneille believe that she was ethically correct in holding that her duty required her to make war with a man she admired because her husband had been killed in fighting him? Or did he simply believe that the best Romans felt that way? That they were a noble but eccentric people, not realists like the French? In *Le Cid* he draws a similar parallel between Chimène's duty to avenge her lover's admittedly justifiable killing of her hateful father in a duel, but there is a definite hint at the end that after a time she may be expected to relent and marry her hero. There is no such hint in *La Mort de Pompée*.

---

*But don't presume you can ever touch my heart. The loss I have suffered is irreparable; the source of my hate is inexpungible; it will last as long as I do. I wish to live and die with my animosity intact. I will admit, however, as a true Roman that my esteem for you equals my hatred, that both are just, and that they demonstrate, one my virtue and the other my duty.

Cinna

This tragedy, whose events are semi-fictional, takes place somewhere in the middle of the reign of Augustus (27 B.C.–A.D. 14), Rome's first and greatest emperor. The former Octavian Caesar is shown at his political zenith, having prevailed over all his enemies and rivals—Brutus, Cassius, Sextus Pompey, Marc Antony, Lepidus—with cruel and effective force. We see him established as the absolute ruler of a consolidated and coordinated empire in a capital which he has transformed from a city of wood and brick to a metropolis of marble.

Yet we see also a weary and disillusioned man. He has summoned his two closest aides, Cinna and Maxime, to ask their advice about abdicating. "Cet empire absolu sur la terre et sur l'onde,"* he confesses to them, is something a man ceases to relish once he has enjoyed it for a time. Auguste will rely wholly on their advice; depending on their word he will remain an emperor or become a private citizen.

Both men, of course, are stunned. They are all the more so in that they have formed a secret conspiracy to assassinate him. But Cinna, pulling himself together, urges the emperor to keep his crown. His motives to kill Auguste are purely personal. He approves of imperial power, seeing nothing but chaos in the

---

*This absolute empire on land and sea.

43

republican form of government that his fellow conspirator seeks to reestablish.

> Et cette liberté, qui lui semble si chère,
> N'est pour Rome, Seigneur, qu'un bien imaginaire.
>
> . . . .
>
> Ces petits souverains qu'il fait pour une année,
> Voyant d'un temps si court leur puissance bornée,
> Des plus heureux desseins font avorter le fruit,
> De peur de le laisser à celui qui les suit.*

Maxime, on the other hand, not only urges the emperor to retire in favor of a more representative government; he adds a veiled threat:

> Vous en avez, Seigneur, des preuves trop certaines:
> On a fait contre vous dix entreprises vaines;
> Peut-être que l'onzième est prête d'éclater,
> Et que ce mouvement qui vous vient agiter
> N'est qu'un avis secret que le ciel vous envoie.†

The emperor inclines to Cinna's argument; he will keep the crown. One cannot help wondering how hard he was to convince.

The plot of the play is simple. All that happens is that Auguste discovers the assassination plan and pardons the conspirators, deciding in the end that there has been too much bloodshed and that the time may have come for mercy. He has based his power on force and terror, which always beget other forces, other terrors, and in the supreme crisis of his life he has learned to define his power in more human terms.

Not all critics have so interpreted Auguste. Another emperor, also the first of his kind in his country, Napoleon, approved of the

---

*And this liberty which seems so precious is for Rome, sir, only an imaginary benefit. . . . These little sovereigns which it makes for a year, seeing their rule confined to so short a period, pluck all the early fruit from public projects for fear of leaving it to their successors.

†The proofs of it, sir, are only too clear. Ten plots have already been discovered against your life; perhaps the eleventh is about to hatch, and your recent misgiving is a warning sent by heaven.

way the famous actor Monvel played the part, indicating to the audience with a shrug that his pardon was only a cynical bid for better public relations. But I think Corneille was trying to tell his audience that the emperor, as we used to say of our presidents, had grown morally in office, that his long reign had endowed him with a wisdom and heart he had not had before.

Certainly Corneille believed that an absolute monarchy was best fitted to govern a country. One must remember that he had seen the worst miseries of religious civil war ended under the iron rule of Richelieu who used the royal power to achieve his ends. The author's admiration for the beneficent rule of Auguste at the end of the play is unmistakably sincere. He has Livie, the empress, intone a kind of paeon to her spouse:

> Rome, avec une joie et sensible et profonde,
> Se démet en vos mains de l'empire du monde;
> Vos royales vertus lui vont trop enseigner
> Que son bonheur consiste à vous faire régner:
> D'une si longue erreur pleinement affranchie,
> Elle n'a plus de vœux que pour la monarchie,
> Vous prépare déjà des temples, des autels,
> Et le ciel une place entre les immortels.*

But one wonders if Corneille is willing to go with her quite as far as she goes when she says:

> Tous les crimes d'État qu'on fait pour la couronne
> Le ciel nous absout alors qu'il nous la donne.
> Et dans le sacré rang où sa faveur l'a mis
> Le passé devient juste et l'avenir permis.†

The women in Corneille tend to do their men one better. Auguste, anyway, has taken the sublime step outside of his own

---

*Rome, with a profound joy, places in your hands the empire of the world. Your royal virtues have convinced her only too well that her welfare consists in having you reign over her. Thoroughly freed now of her longtime error, she has no further use for any government but monarchy, and she is already preparing for you her temples and altars and a place among the immortals.

†Heaven forgives the crimes we commit for the crown, and in the sacred rank where her favor has placed us the past becomes just and the future permissible.

ego to make himself a true ruler of mankind. This is *gloire* at its highest point.

The two conspirators enjoy less of this quality. Their motives are not pure. Both are contaminated by their love for the beautiful and brave Émilie who is consumed with a passion to avenge the killing of her father by the emperor. Cinna is really motivated *only* by his love for her, in his case at least, returned. He has some old family grudges against the emperor, but they are perfunctory. When Émilie names the emperor's head as the price for her hand, Cinna impulsively swears to do the deed and feels himself bound by his oath, even after he has become convinced by Auguste's willingness to abdicate that his proposed victim is a great and selfless ruler. He feels his *gloire* to be at stake; it requires a murder, even against his conscience. He is a kind of Horace gone mad; he has no choice but to obey his mistress, even if he must kill himself afterwards. He tells her:

> Vous me faites priser ce qui me déshonore,
> Vous me faites haïr ce que mon âme adore;
> Vous me faites répandre un sang pour qui je dois
> Exposer tout le mien et mille et mille fois;
> Vous le voulez, j'y cours, ma parole est donnée;
> Mais ma main, aussitôt contre mon sein tournée,
> Aux mânes d'un tel prince immolant votre amant,
> A mon crime forcé joindra mon châtiment,
> Et par cette action dans l'autre confondue,
> Recouvrera ma gloire aussitôt que perdue.*

Did Corneille really think his protagonist could rescue his *gloire* by a suicide following a murder? I cannot think so, though it does make us question the emperor's supposed great wisdom in continuing to entrust this rash and hotheaded fellow with a vital government post even after all is known.

---

*You make me prize what dishonors me; you make me hate that which my heart adores; you want me me to shed blood that I should save at the price of my own a thousand times over. You wish it, and I obey. My word is given. But my knife, immediately afterward turned on myself and immolating your lover to the shade of the dead prince, will unite my punishment to my forced crime and revive my glory as fast as it has been lost.

Cinna's co-conspirator is much more sympathetic, at least to modern readers, at the start, for he has joined in the plot only as a means of restoring representative government and is perfectly willing to spare the emperor's life if he will abdicate. But Corneille, who must have felt about democracy as we have about communism, seems to connect Maxime's political views with the bad character with which he now endows him. Maxime becomes the villain of the piece, betraying Cinna in a desperate effort to abduct the heroine who despises him. We can never believe that Cinna will give more than lip service to the generous emperor's injunction in the last act that he must forgive Maxime.

The play, better read today than acted, is a brilliant and beautiful dialogue on the subject of political power, but the poet in the end does nothing to reconcile his idealistic picture of Augustus's presumably golden reign with the sorry state of affairs that followed under his immediate successors. Tiberius, Caligula, Claudius, and Nero are as familiar to us as they were to Corneille's audiences, and he should have at least qualified his encomiums of the founder of the imperial line by explaining why so great a sovereign had allowed his relatives to destroy themselves so completely in internecine rivalry that only the rottenest twigs on the family tree survived to rule. Corneille would have probably admitted this defect in the system of the Caesars, but he might have argued that it had been corrected in the monarchies of his own era, and that therefore, as a champion of royalty, he didn't have to be concerned with it.

In the first place, he could have pointed out, the principle of the sovereign's being allowed to choose his successor from among his descendants, direct or collateral, had been done away with, and a strict stirpital order established. A dauphin of France inherited from his father regardless of his age or capacity. And in the second, the lives of the princes of the blood were sacred; the killing of one was followed by execution with appalling tortures. And finally, the nobles of the realm were essentially emasculated; they became ornaments in the court and were rewarded with titles and riches proportionate to their utility to the crown. The Roman imperial system, with its constant assassination of emperors and its almost annual crop of imperial claimants, had set an example for the ages on how *not* to regulate the succession to the crown. Happily for Corneille, he lived only to see the glories of the Sun King and not the sad defeats at the end of that long reign.

Britannicus

Corneille chose not to compose a drama about the emperor who, if not the most famous, is certainly the most infamous of Roman history. There was no *gloire* in the reign of Nero, which is probably why it failed to appeal to Corneille; it was the time only of a monster and his toadies. Britannicus, the son and heir of Claudius, who was thrust out of the succession by the maneuvering of his stepmother, Agrippina, in favor of her own son, Nero, was only fourteen when he died and not qualified to be the protagonist of a drama. Racine, however, chose to add enough years to his age to make him a hero, and to add a heroine to his play in the shape of Junie, a princess of the Augustan family, who loves and is beloved by him. The twenty-four hours of the tragedy encompass the murder of Britannicus, at Nero's order, in the year 55 A.D.

Yet Britannicus, shown as very young, almost still a lad, and at all times the helpless captive of his imperial stepbrother, duped even by his confidant, Narcisse, who is secretly Nero's agent, is hardly able to be more than a titular hero. He is attractively and even recklessly defiant, but there is not much he can do in his precarious position. The play is about Nero and what is going on in Nero's mind and soul.

This is where Racine *complements* Corneille. We really need both playwrights. After reading a certain number of Corneille's tragedies one feels the need of Racine. After the loud and even

49

at times bombastic arguments between duty-obsessed characters about the demands made on them by the state, the king, the church, the spouse, the lover, it may be a relief to turn to the people of Racine who tear *themselves* apart, whose conflicts seem born in their own strife-ridden hearts. In *Britannicus* the tragedy is not in the Roman empire; it is in the emperor himself.

Racine stands alone among French classic dramatists in treating the tragic unities of time, place, and action not as hurdles that must be overcome, but as essentials to the play. Each moment in time contains the past and the future; the exciting experience is to choose the moment just before the future reveals its nature. The evil in Nero was unknown to his court in the first three benevolent years of his reign; he was the idol of the army and of the populace. True, his crowning had been at the expense of Britannicus, but the Romans were accustomed to irregular successions. And then, in a single day, in the poisoning of his stepbrother, Nero embarked on a course from which there was no return. But, as only his mother knew, the moral cancer, undetected even by its victim, had been slowly developing from his early years.

As the play opens we learn that the emperor has taken the startling step of having Junie abducted from her home by his guards and brought to the palace. Yet it appears that Néron's intentions are at least quasi-honorable. He has fallen violently in love with her and wishes to make her his empress after he has divorced the barren Octavie. But Agrippine reads more into the emperor's expressed purpose than that. She sees his inner rapacity at last surfacing. And she deplores it largely because she sees Junie as a greater potential danger to her maternal domination than the placid Octavie and wishes to marry her to Britannicus and hold the couple over Néron's head as a threat to his imperium should he ever try to thrust his mother aside. All this she announces haughtily to Burrhus, her son's chief minister, reminding him that she is the "fille, femme, sœur et mère de vos maîtres."* True enough; she was the daughter of Germanicus, the wife of Claudius, the sister of Caligula, and the mother of Nero.

---

*Daughter , wife, sister and mother of your masters.

In the superb lines of his confession to Narcisse of his love for Junie Néron reveals the latent sadism of his character:

> Cette nuit je l'ai vue arriver en ces lieux,
> Triste, levant au ciel ses yeux mouillés de larmes,
> Qui brillaient au travers des flambeaux et des armes;
> Belle, sans ornements, dans le simple appareil
> D'une beauté qu'on vient d'arracher au sommeil.
> Que veux-tu? Je ne sais si cette négligence,
> Les ombres, les flambeaux, les cris et le silence,
> Et le farouche aspect de ses fiers ravisseurs,
> Relevaient de ses yeux les timides douceurs.*

He gives himself totally away a moment later: "J'aimais jusqu'à ses pleurs que je faisais couler."†

When he discovers that he cannot bend Junie to his will, that nothing can win her away from Britannicus, he arranges to have the latter poisoned but is momentarily dissuaded by Agrippine, who threatens to incite a rebellion against him if Britannicus and Junie are not liberated and her own powerful position in court reaffirmed. However, another conference with Narcisse, his evil genius, reconciles him to his lethal plan. Britannicus is duly poisoned at a public banquet, but Junie escapes to the sanctuary of the vestal virgins.

The greatest scenes in the play are those in which the arrogant and ruthless Agrippine, a magnificent study in criminal ambition and daring, seeks to impose her will on her sultry, cowering, but already matricidally minded son. She flings in his teeth all the crimes she has committed to win him the throne, including the seduction of Claudius, her own uncle.

> Quand de Britannicus la mère condamnée
> Laissa de Claudius disputer l'hyménée,

---

*The night that I saw her arrive here, so sad, lifting to the sky her eyes brimmed with tears but still shining amid the torches and flashing arms, radiant, unadorned, in the simple nightwear of a beauty who has been torn from her sleep—what can I say? I don't know if it was her disarray, or the shadows, or the torches, or the cries, or the silence, or the fierce aspect of the arresting guards that so intensified for me the sweet timidity of those eyes.

†I loved the very tears that I caused her to shed.

> Parmi tant de beautés qui briguèrent son choix,
> Qui de ses affranchis mendièrent les voix,
> Je souhaitai son lit, dans la seule pensée,
> De vous laisser au trône où je serai placée.[*]

And when in the end she realizes that, with the murder of Britannicus, Néron is irredeemably launched on a career of bloodshed and tyranny which will surely encompass even his mother's downfall and death, she gives him dire warning of what his own downfall will be.

> Mais j'espère qu'enfin le ciel, las de tes crimes,
> Ajoutera ta perte à tant d'autres victimes,
> Qu'après t'être couvert de leur sang et du mien,
> Tu te verra forcé de répandre le tien;
> Et ton nom paraîtra, dans la race future,
> Aux plus cruels tyrans une cruelle injure.
> Voilà ce que mon cœur présage de toi.
> Adieu, tu peux sortir.[†]

---

[*]When Britannicus's repudiated mother left Claudius open to matrimonial bids, and all the beauties of the court sought to purchase in their favor the voices of his corruptible freedmen, I sought his bed, with the sole idea of leaving you the throne on which I planned to be seated.

[†]But I hope one day that the heavens, weary of your crimes, will add you to the long list of your victims, and that after covering yourself with blood, including even your mother's, you will see yourself at last forced to shed your own, and that the coupling of your name with theirs in the future will be a cruel insult to the cruelest of tyrants. That is what my heart presages for you. Farewell. You may leave me now.

Othon

Corneille's Othon, the emperor Otho who reigned for three months in A.D. 69, the year of the three emperors, seems to vary considerably from his historical model, but a close comparison may show a basic consistency.

"Thus," as Seymour Van Santvoord in *The House of Caesar* (1901) describes the death of Nero in that fatal year, "miserably perished the last of the Caesars—112 years after that other death at the foot of Pompey's statue had at last made possible the imperial system and marked the elevation of its one great ruling family of which Nero was the last distorted product. During that interval we have seen 65 Caesars by birth or marriage put to death by the sovereign power; while of all those born in the Julian line, except such as perished in infancy, history tells us of only five who died from natural causes."

Tacitus has this description of the aftermath: "Rome was devastated by conflagrations in which her most ancient shrines were consumed and the very Capitol fired by citizens' hands. Sacred rites were defiled; there were adulteries in high places. The sea was filled with exiles, its cliffs made foul with the bodies of the dead. In Rome there was more awful cruelty. High birth, wealth, the refusal or acceptance of office—all gave ground for accusations, and virtues caused the greatest ruin" (*Tacitus, The Histories,* with an English translation by Clifford H. Moore [1925]).

The new emperor, Galba, a soldier, but an ancient one, chosen by other soldiers, pronounced the new way of selecting the chief of state, whose absolute rule was considered necessary in so vast and scattered an empire: "Under Tiberius, Gaius (Caligula), and Claudius, we Romans were the heritage, so to speak, of one family; the fact that we emperors are now beginning to be chosen will be for all a kind of liberty." This vaticination belongs in what the *New Yorker* magazine used to call "Department of Cloudy Crystal Ball."

The new emperor, verging on senility, soon became the property of a trio of designing and unscrupulous ministers: Vinius, Lacus, and Martian, the last a freedman of Galba's. Left out of this inner group was Otho, an ex-friend of Nero, though as the efficient governor of Lusitania, to which province he had been exiled so that the treacherous Nero could make love to Otho's wife, he had actively championed Galba's cause. His discontent at the new emperor's ingratitude led to his ultimate rebellion, the assassination of Galba, and his own coronation. But after a reign of only three months his troops were defeated by Vitellius who became the "third" emperor of the doomed year, and Otho committed suicide.

According to Tacitus, Otho's youth was spent in idleness and dissipation. He was a companion of Nero in the latter's debauches until Nero coveted Otho's wife, Poppaea, decreed a divorce, and made her his empress. In the early days of Galba's reign he brooded over his injustices, past and present. "Otho's mind was not effeminate like his body. His intimate freedmen and slaves, who had more license than prevails in private houses, constantly held before his eager eyes Nero's luxurious court, his adulteries, his many marriages and other royal vices, exhibiting them as his own if he only dared to take them."

When Galba came to dine with Otho, his host would "tip" each cohort of the escorting imperial guard with one hundred sesterces, knowing well that the soldiers would immediately contrast such openhandedness with their sovereign's notorious stinginess.

Piso, a nobleman of ancient lineage now adopted as the

emperor's successor on the advice of the three conniving ministers, tried to counteract the disappointed Otho's tactics in a public address to the guards. In Tacitus's words: "Was it by his bearing and gait or by his womanish dress that he deserved the throne? They are deceived who are imposed upon by extravagance under the garb of generosity. He will know how to ruin; he will not know how to give. Adulteries and revelries and gatherings of women occupy his thoughts; these he considers the prerogatives of imperial power."

One wonders if the guards would have been quite so keen about a man of womanish dress. Nor is one entirely convinced by Suetonius's statement that Otho had his body hair plucked out and wore a very convincing wig. But I have little doubt that Tacitus's description of how he ultimately incited the troops to revolt is accurate: "Otho did not fail in his part; he stretched out his hands and did obeisance to the common soldiers, threw kisses and played the slave to secure the master's place."

But after the Praetorian guards had dragged old Galba from his chair, cut off his head, and proclaimed Otho lord of the known world, the new emperor, according to Tacitus, "ordered his life as befitted the imperial position," putting away his old habits and conducting himself as a model chief of state. But it was too late. Half of Rome simply dreaded all the more what they regarded as the inevitable return of his old vices. Vitellius, a general in the north who had never recognized the usurper, led his army on Rome and defeated Otho in what was a disastrous but not necessarily a decisive battle. Otho, however, nobly determined to put a stop to this bloody civil war and commanded his men to join the attackers and make peace. He then fell on his sword in his tent. Like the thane of Cawdor in *Macbeth*, nothing in his life became him like the leaving it.

I see Othon in Corneille's drama as a well-built but slender man, younger looking than his thirty-seven years, with a pale, noble countenance verging on the beautiful and crisply curled, shining blond hair, finely dressed (if a touch too elegant), with easy, winning manners, peculiarly attractive to women and having a way with crowds but evoking an occasional sneer from a macho or would-be macho type. His popularity with Néron is evidence of his charm and adaptability, and the sudden emergence of administrative talents that he demonstrated in Lusitania has been seen in other brilliant gilded butterflies when their lives of pleasure have been curtailed.

As the play opens, finding himself outside the inner circle of power, he has sought to cultivate the protection of at least one of the insidious three, Vinius, by paying his court to the latter's daughter, Plautine. But what started as politics has turned into love. He explains to his confidant why he has had to operate in this fashion:

> Ceux qu'on voit s'étonner de ce nouvel amour
> N'ont jamais bien conçu ce que c'est que la cour.
> Un homme tel que moi jamais ne s'en détache;
> Il n'est point de retraite ou d'ombre que le cache;
> Et si du souverain la faveur n'est pour lui,
> Il faut ou qu'il périsse, ou qu'il prend un appui.[*]

Voltaire, whose opinion is sometimes hard to follow but is always fascinating, found Othon's following four lines, describing the voracity of the governing trio, the most sublime in all of Corneille:

> Je les voyais tous trois se hâter sous un maître
> Qui, chargé d'un long âge, a peu de temps à l'être,
> Et tous trois à l'envi s'empresser ardemment
> A qui dévorerait ce règne d'un moment.[†]

The spectacle of an aging ruler isolated by an ambitious clique is not unusual. A brigadier general on MacArthur's staff in Tokyo told me that, in his bitter opinion, General Courtney Whitney had

---

[*]Those who are astonished at this new love of mine have never clearly understood what a court is. A man like myself can never get away from it. There is no place where he can hide, and if he's not in the good graces of the emperor, he either perishes or finds a strong support.

[†]I watched the three of them scampering about under an aged sovereign to amass what riches and power they could in this reign of a moment.

transformed a military headquarters into an oriental court. And the given rank of a clique member is of no significance; access to the chief's ear is all. Harry Hopkins had a only a simple table desk to work on, but it was in FDR's White House. As Martian, the base freedman of the emperor (Corneille like Racine is very snobbish about freedmen; they can never lose the taint of their former chains), explains to the noble Plautine, whom he has the temerity to court, though he knows that she loves Othon:

> Madame, en quelque rang que vous avez pu naître,
> C'est beaucoup d'avoir l'oreille du grand maître.*

Martian deludes himself that he has a chance with the disdainful Plautine, because Galba, in one of his flimflams, has decided to name as his successor the man to whom he will bestow the hand of his niece Camille, and Vinius, in the greater interest of his faction, has insisted that Othon abandon his suit to his daughter and offer the merchandise of his affections to this now more promising party. Plautine, seeing that this is the best policy for her beloved, has unselfishly given him up, even going so far as to threaten to wed the odious Martian if Othon refuses. Her father suggests that Othon might dump Camille once he is emperor and return to his true love, but Plautine rejects the idea as ignoble. She will not have him kick over the ladder by which he has climbed.

Of all the characters in the play Plautine is the only one of unblemished integrity. As Othon truly says of her, "son cœur est noble et grand."† Toward the end, when her always-bargaining father proposes that they hedge their bets on Othon by keeping in with Piso who might marry her if Othon should lose his coup d'état, she indignantly excoriates him. Perhaps Corneille is telling us that in the Rome of 69 A.D. only a woman is capable of *gloire*.

The position of a hero in the whispering galleries of a dark and intriguing court is a difficult one successfully to dramatize. *Othon* makes better reading than staging. The protagonist must either play the role of toady to the supreme dictator or die resisting

---

*Madam, in whatever rank you happen to have been born, it is much to have the ear of the sovereign.

†her heart is great and noble.

him. If he does the latter, the play is over. Racine faced the same problem with the eponymous hero of *Bajazet,* a prisoner in the harem of the absent sultan, who must make love to the all-powerful sultana, Roxane, in order to gain her support for a rebellion and save his own and his secretly betrothed's threatened lives. If he does so effectively he will appear a hypocrite, and if he does so ineffectively (which is what happens) he will appear an ass. Only the fine fury of the unconvinced Roxane saves the play.

Corneille gave himself an even harder task. After Othon has reluctantly commenced his courtship of Camille, Galba does another flip and names Piso his successor. If Camille refuses the new heir—which she does—she will get nothing. She has now no further political value, and Othon can return to Plautine. But his way of breaking off with Camille is odious. He pretends that she must not refuse Piso; Othon cannot stand between her and the throne.

> Quoi donc, Madame? Othon vous coûterait l'empire?
> Il sait mieux ce qu'il vaut, et n'est pas d'un tel prix
> Qu'il le faille acheter par ce noble mépris.
> Il se doit opposer à cet effort d'estime
> Où s'abaisse pour lui ce cœur trop magnanime,
> Et par un même effort de magnanimité,
> Rendre une âme si haute au trône mérité.*

Camille is not deceived. She replies pathetically: "Vous n'aimez que l'empire, et je n'aimais que vous."†

Corneille is, as ever, a realist. Othon behaves as many good men would behave. He might be a member of the CIA, intent on bringing down a third world dictatorship and not too squeamish about who must be sacrificed in the process. Yet he expresses, perhaps a bit too much, how vastly he would prefer death to what he has to do. He sees clearly enough how the situation has

---

*What are you saying, madam? That Othon could cost you the empire? He knows better what he's worth, and that he's hardly the price of a crown so nobly disdained. He must certainly oppose your generous condescension and restore your lofty soul to the throne it deserves.

†You love only the empire, and I love only you.

demeaned him. "Je n'ai donc qu'à mourir." "Courons à la mort." "Que ne m'est il permis d'éviter par ma mort . . . ?"[*]

For, of course, it is his *gloire* that he wishes vainly to save from this stifling pit. He urges Plautine at one point:

> Périssons, périssons, madame, l'un pour l'autre,
> Avec toute ma gloire, avec toute la vôtre.
> Pour nous faire un trépas dont les dieux soient jaloux,
> Rendez-vous toute à moi, comme moi tout à vous.[†]

One wonders if Corneille had read *King Lear:*

> Upon such sacrifices, my Cordelia,
> The gods themselves throw incense.

The action of the play culminates in a deadly turmoil of crisscrossing treacheries in which Galba and his three ministers are all slaughtered, and Othon is raised to the throne. But even in the end the unhappy new emperor has been unable to achieve anything for himself—he is borne to the imperial palace reluctantly on the shoulders of the triumphant guards. The curtain descends on a somber scene, with Plautine weeping for her father and Othon speaking darkly of "ce malheureux jour."[‡] Corneille's audience, trained in Roman history, would be aware that his reign would last but three months.

---

[*]There's nothing left for me but to die. Let us rush to death. Why can't I avoid, by death . . . ?

[†]Let us die, madam, one for the other, I possessed of all my glory, and you of all of yours; let us make the gods jealous of our ending. Give yourself altogether to me, as I to you.

[‡]this unhappy day

Tite et Bérénice

Voltaire in his preface to *Tite et Bérénice* tells the story of the play's supposed origin. The lovely Henrietta of England, wife of Philippe d'Orléans, brother of Louis XIV, was in love with the king and he with her. This heady romance between the handsome and heroic young sovereign and his charming sister-in-law titillated the court, nor did it probably much bother the former's dull Spanish queen nor the latter's promiscuously homo-sexual spouse. But "Madame," as Henrietta was known, and the "Roi Soleil," as her lover was soon to be dubbed, came to see their mutual passion as detrimental to the dignity of the royal family and brought it to an end. Henrietta, however, thought that such a triumph of mind over heart was worthy of being commemorated in a poetic drama, and she sent the Marquis de Dangeau to the great Corneille and to his young rival in the theatre, Jean Racine, without telling either he had called on the other, to suggest that majesty would be pleased to see a play based on the story of the Roman emperor Titus (A.D. 79–81) and Bérénice, queen of Palestine, who terminated their tempestuous love affair and gave up their marriage plans in deference to Rome's obsessional hostility to foreign royalty.

Both poets promptly complied, and both plays were produced in 1670. Racine's was a smash hit, and Corneille's was a flop, nor has there been much question in the opinion of posterity that the contemporary audiences were correct in their judgment. Voltaire

61

even included Racine's tragedy in his edition of Corneille to show where the older playwright had gone wrong.

It was largely in the plot. Racine in his play *Bérénice* knew just how to strip a story to its dramatic essentials which were these: Titus, raised to the crown by the death of his father, Vespasien, sees nothing in the way of his marrige to his beloved Bérénice but his duty to the people who adore him. This duty, however, he comes to view as sacred, and he sends Bérénice back to Palestine after some tearful scenes. How is a dramatist to stretch that over five acts? Racine did it simply by the introduction of a third character, Antiochus, king of Comagène, who is Titus's best friend and his secret rival for Bérénice's love. Antiochus's colloquies with the emperor and with the queen bring out every angle of the tragic situation and supply the dramatic tension required.

Corneille, on the other hand, rambled all over the place. Dissatisfied with the bare bones of the story, he added the romance (if that is the word for it) between Domitian, the emperor's coldhearted brother and eventual successor, and Domitie, a haughty lady of quasi-imperial birth who aspires to be empress and will marry, despite her alleged sentiment for Domitian, anyone who will make her that. As the play opens Tite has actually sent Bérénice away and has engaged himself to Domitie, persuaded by his councillors that the latter, if refused, will ally herself to his untrusted brother and foment a dangerous rebellion. Bérénice returns, furious at the news, but shows herself willing to accept the emperor's marriage to another provided it be not Domitie, of whose looks and power she is jealous. Domitian now intervenes to extract Domitie from her engagement (though she has no wish to be released) by informing his brother that if he marries her, *he* will marry Bérénice, knowing that Tite will not abide the idea of his true love in the arms of another. The general confusion is at last cleared up by Tite's decision never to marry at all, to send Bérénice back to her own kingdom, and to satisfy Domitie and Domitian by advising them to content themselves with a present wedding to each other and to await his demise to inherit the empire.

This awkward plot makes four petty persons out of the four main characters. Tite, the mighty conqueror of the Mideast, the lord of the world, is shown as trembling before a silly woman's political threats; Bérénice, as ridiculously insisting that Tite choose a dowdy as his consort; Domitian, as a traitor to his brother and to Rome; and Domitie as a cold and spiteful egotist.

There is no love in a play that was supposed to be all about it. Voltaire commented that neither great men—Alexander, Scipio, Caesar—nor vile ones—Caligula, Nero, Domitian—should be shown in love on the stage because love degrades the former and appears grotesque in the latter. I don't think Tite is degraded, but certainly Domitian is grotesque. And in Domitie love is nothing more than an itch that hampers her real passion, ambition. As she frankly avers:

> Et je n'ai point une âme à se laisser charmer
> Du ridicule honneur de savoir bien aimer.
> La passion du trône est seule toujours belle,
> Seule à qui l'âme doive une ardeur immortelle.*

But I have argued that Corneille, if rarely romantic, is almost always realistic, which is what makes him produce characters who, however odd they may appear on the stage as not conforming to known theatrical types, are nonetheless, if rightly viewed, recognizable men and women. Have we not all known women like Domitie? And she might be effective, too, like the monstrous Cléopâtre in Corneille's *Rodogune* who asks her son to kill his beloved, if she were balanced with some nobler characters. But here there are none. Only Albin, the cynical but clear-sighted confidant of Domitian, voices our reaction when Domitian complains to him that Domitie loves nobody but herself:

> Seigneur, s'il m'est permis de parler librement,
> Dans toute la nature aime-t-on autrement?
> L'amour-propre est la source en nous de tous les autres;

---

*I haven't the kind of soul that allows itself to be flattered by the foolish art of knowing how to love well. The love of a crown alone is beautiful to me. For that I have an immortal ardor.

63

C'en est le sentiment qui forme tous les nôtres.
Lui seul allume, éteint, ou change nos désirs:
Les objets de nos vœux le sont de nos plaisirs.
Vous-même, qui brûlez d'une ardeur si fidèle,
Aimez-vous Domitie, ou vos plaisirs en elle?
Et quand vous aspirez à des liens si doux,
Est-ce pour l'amour d'elle ou pour l'amour de vous?*

One can only agree with Voltaire when he equates with comedy some of Corneille's bickering scenes in which insults are briskly traded. Tite, it is true, is given some wonderful lines, as when he complains that he imposes a harsh rule on himself:

Maître de l'univers sans l'être de moi-même,
Je suis le seul rebelle a ce pouvoir extrême;†

or when he warns his brother that civil wars are always the bloodiest:

De ceux qu'unit le sang plus douces sont les chaînes,
Plus leur désunion met d'aigreur dans leurs haines;
L'offense en est plus rude, et le courroux plus grand,
La suite plus barbare, et l'effet plus sanglant.
La nature en fureur s'abandonne à tout faire,
Et cinquante ennemis sont moins haïs qu'un frère.‡

Fine verses, however, do not make a play. There are fulminating passages in Shakespeare's *Timon of Athens* as powerful as any uttered by King Lear on the heath, but a bad plot spoils all.

---

*Sir, if I may speak frankly, does anyone love any other way? Self-love is the source of all our loves. It is the emotion from which all others are born. It and it alone enlightens or extinguishes our desires. The objects of all our vows are simply our pleasures. Yourself, sir, who burn with so faithful an ardor, do you really love Domitia or your own delight in her? And when you yearn to be intimate with her, is it for love of her or love of yourself?

†Master of the universe, but not of myself, I'm the sole rebel in my own domain.

‡The closer we are united in blood, the more bitter is our disunion. The offense becomes greater, the ire sharper, the ensuing conflict bloodier and more barbarous. Our nature explodes in hate, and fifty foes are less hated than one brother.

Perhap the audience in 1670 could derive some satisfaction in recalling that the Domitie of history not only married Domitian but joined in the plot to assassinate him.

Poor Corneille must have had too good an ear not to have recognized that his rival had written a masterpiece. With a minimum of words Racine could convey the plight and despair of each of the three protagonists. Antiochus expresses perfectly to his confidant the bleak experience of being liked but not loved by the woman he silently adores:

> Que vous dirai-je enfin? je fuis des yeux distraits
> Qui me voyant toujours ne me voyait jamais.*

Racine's Titus tells us just how agonizing it will be to inform his mistress that he is quitting her when he describes the totality of her devotion:

> Sans avoir en aimant d'objet que son amour,
> Étrangère dans Rome et inconnue à la cour,
> Elle passe ses jours, Paulin, sans rien prétendre
> Que quelque heure à me voir, et le reste à m'attendre.†

And Bérénice touches us deeply when she wishes that her and Titus's positions were reversed so that she might prove to him the depth and disinterestedness of her love:

> Ah! plût au ciel que, sans blesser ta gloire,
> Un rival plus puissant voulût tenter ma foi,
> Et pût mettre à mes pieds plus d'empires que toi,
> Que de sceptres sans nombre il pût payer ma flamme,
> Que ton amour n'eût rien à donner que ton âme;
> C'est alors, cher Titus, qu'aime, victorieux,
> Tu verrais de quel prix ton cœur est à mes yeux!‡

---

*What can I tell you? I flee eyes that look upon me but never see me.

†With no interest in life but loving me, a stranger in Rome, unknown at court, her days are occupied solely with my visits or waiting for them.

‡Ah, would to God, saving your glory, that a greater rival might test my faithfulness and offer me more kingdoms than you, seek to bribe me with more scepters, and that you had nothing to offer but your heart—it would be then, dear Titus, that you would see how highly I prized it!

Finally, however well known they may be, I cannot resist quoting the famous lines of her wail at their parting:

> Pour jamais! Ah! Seigneur, songez vous en vous-même
> Combien ce mot cruel est affreux quand on aime?
> Dans un mois, dans un an, comment souffrirons nous
> Seigneur, que tant de mers me séparent de vous?
> Que le jour recommence et que le jour finisse
> Sans que jamais Titus puisse voir Bérénice,
> Sans que de tout le jour je puisse voir Titus?*

Corneille never wrote anything quite like that. Perhaps he did not feel that love was really compatible with the rise and fall of the Roman Empire. But he would have certainly agreed with Racine's estimation, expressed by Titus to Bérénice, of how an abdication of the throne in the interests of love would have degraded the sovereign:

> Vous-même rougiriez de ma lâche conduite:
> Vous verriez à regret marcher à votre suite
> Un indigne empereur, sans empire, sans cour,
> Vil spectacle aux humains des faiblesses d'amour.†

This might have been, according to Mary McCarthy, a perfect description of the sad peregrinations of the duke and duchess of Windsor in our own time.

---

*Forever! Ah, sir, consider how cruel that word is to lovers! In a month, in a year, how shall we abide having so many seas between us? How can we allow the days to end and start over if Titus can never see his Berenice—if she can never see her Titus?

†You yourself would blush at such cowardly conduct. You would scorn to see in your entourage an unworthy emperor, with neither empire nor court, vile specimen of the feebleness of love.

Polyeucte

T he first of the Roman tragedies to take up the issue of Christianity is *Polyeucte,* which is laid in the short reign of Decius (249–251 A.D.), who initiated a severe persecution of the rapidly growing sect. In his *History of the Decline and Fall of the Roman Empire* (1776–1788), Gibbon, who was always inclined to denigrate the early church and minimize the sufferings of the martyrs, quotes Origen to the effect that "in the immense city of Alexandria and under the rigorous persecution of Decius" only ten men and seven women paid for their faith with their lives, and that "four Roman emperors, with their families, their favorites and their adherents, perished by the sword in the space of ten years during which the bishop of Carthage guided by his authority and eloquence the African church."

Corneille, a devout Christian educated by Jesuits, obviously took a more stringent view of what had happened, but, in any case, the imperial justicers may have been less lenient in Armenia, where the action of the play occurs, than in Africa. The hero is faced with death as early as the second act. What is fascinating to a modern reader is how easily and convincingly Corneille fits the tumultuous actions of his drama into the twenty-four hours allowed. For that was more than enough time, as he makes one see it, for the deity to transmit to a true believer the explosive power of divine grace. And grace is what the play is all about.

Polyeucte, an Armenian noble of royal blood and the chosen son-in-law of the Roman governor Félix, has just been baptized, as the curtain rises, in the outlawed faith. This will create a grave problem for his pagan wife, Pauline, but she has another that will worry her still more. In obediently wedding Polyeucte, at her father's behest, she has had to suppress her love for Sévère, a Roman soldier whose indigence has disqualified him for her hand. Sévère has since been reported dead in battle, but he has suddenly turned up in Armenia, not only alive and still enamored of her, but the all-powerful favorite of the emperor as well. Finding that she has a husband, he is too much a gentleman to resume his pursuit, but she, on her side, is horrified to discover that, despite all her desperate determination to be faithful to Polyeucte, her old passion is still dangerously active.

Polyeucte's attitude is wonderfully interesting. He professes to adore his wife, but he has already resolved to smash the graven images of the heathen gods at a public sacrifice attended by the governor, and, knowing that he will not long survive this act of sacrilege, he finds Sévère an admirable solution to the problem of his bereft widow.

Can one differ with an author as to the degree of a character's emotional commitment? *Does* Polyeucte really love Pauline? In *On Racine* (1963; trans. Richard Howard, 1964), Roland Barthes wrote of Titus and Bérénice in Racine's *Bérénice:* "It is Bérénice who desires Titus. Titus is linked to Bérénice only by habit." I believe that if Racine could have read that, he would have strongly denied it. I have little doubt that he conceived of his hero as a man deeply in love. But that does not mean that Barthes is necessarily wrong or even that he is faulting Racine as an artist. Perhaps the playwright had built better than he knew, creating a man who believes that he is in love and who talks and acts as if he were in love, but who *we,* more detached than Racine, can see is really not.

In the same way it might be argued that Polyeucte, unbeknownst to himself, has only a cool affection for his wife. Could he otherwise aver in a soliloquy:

> Monde, pour moi tu n'as plus rien :
> Je porte en un cœur tout chrétien
> Une flamme toute divine ;

> Et je ne regarde Pauline
> Que comme un obstacle à mon bien.*

And when he is led off to his execution, his last words to her are hardly consoling: he offers her the choice of a life with her old lover or a martyr's death with himself.

> Je vous l'ai déjà dit, et vous le dis encore,
> Vivez avec Sévère, ou mourez avec moi.
> Je ne méprise point vos pleurs ni votre foi;
> Mais, de quoi que pour vous notre amour
>   m'entretienne,
> Je ne vous connais plus, si vous n'êtes chrétienne.†

Of course, it could be argued on the other side that Pauline does little enough to attract his love. She is always, like Sophonisbe, throwing in his teeth how great is his debt to her for having, in marrying him, overcome her passion for Sévère.

> Que t'ai-je fait, cruel, pour être ainsi traitée,
> Et pour me reprocher, au mépris de ma foi,
> Un amour si puissant que j'ai vaincu pour toi?
> Vois, pour te faire vaincre un si fort adversaire,
> Quels efforts à moi-même il a fallu me taire,
> Quels combats j'ai donnés pour te donner un cœur.‡

But I doubt that Corneille found these lines quite as shrill and ungracious as we may. I think he admired Pauline for subduing her earlier love and found it natural (as indeed it would be for some) to seek credit for it. One of the achievements of his technique is that we do not really very much care what Polyeucte and Pauline feel for each other. They are both forcefully alive, he illuminated and solely motivated by the gift of grace and she strangely dignified by her

---

*World, you are nothing to me; my heart is all Christian. I burn with a divine flame, and I see in Pauline only an obstacle to my salvation.

†I've said it once, and I'll say it again: live with Severus or die with me. I despise neither your tears nor your fidelity, but whatever our love may say in your favor, if you're not a Christian, I know you not.

‡What have I done to deserve such treatment? Do you hold against me the powerful love that I overcame to give myself to you? You should have seen what efforts that cost me, what struggles I had to undergo to free my heart for you.

puritanical obsession over her inexpugnable pre-marital passion and her dread that it may drag her into adultery.

To return to the main theme of the play, does it matter whether or not we believe in grace and miracles? Or if Corneille did? I happen to believe that he did. Millions have, and their faith has played a mighty part in history. His picture of the role of such faith in the early years of Christianity is both interesting and exciting. Baptism, desecration of the old gods, and martyrdom, all come to Polyeucte within a space of twenty-four hours, nor does he suffer from a single qualm, a single doubt. All to him is joy.

The friend who converted him, Néarque, sees God's grace, accorded in baptism, as given at its most powerful.

> Vous sortez du baptême, et ce qui vous anime,
> C'est sa grâce qu'en vous n'affaiblit aucun crime;
> Comme encor toute entière elle agit pleinement,
> Et tout semble possible a son feu véhément.[*]

Indeed the grace is strong. Polyeucte cannot wait a minute before rushing to destroy the idols. God has favored him signally, he declares: the doors of heaven are opening even as the doors of the baptistry close behind him. Poor Néarque is appalled at what is so suddenly expected of him. "Dieu même a craint la mort!" he cries.[†] But Polyeucte retorts:

> Il s'est offert pourtant: suivons ce saint effort;
> Dressons-lui des autels sur des morceaux d'idoles.
> Il faut (je me souviens encor de vos paroles)
> Négliger, pour lui plaire, et femme, et biens, et rang,
> Exposer pour sa gloire et verser tout son sang.[‡]

Some critics have opined that even Corneille was aware that he was painting the protrait of a religious extremist whose lofty stan-

---

[*]You have just emerged from the baptistry; that is what inspires you. This fresh new grace is untainted by any sin; it now operates at its fullest, and you feel capable of anything.

[†]God himself feared death!

[‡]Yet he offered his body to it; let us follow his saintly example. Let us rear him an altar with the shards of these idols. We must (as I recall your own words) neglect everything else to please him: wife, goods, and rank, and be ready to shed our blood for his glory.

dards of godliness and self-sacrifice were not meant to be followed by the multitude; that, as T. S. Eliot was to endorse in *The Cocktail Party,* there were different roles for saints such as Celia Copplestone, whose destiny was to become a missionary and be crucified by savages, and the Chamberlaynes, who had only to lead decent Christian lives in a world of eponymous entertainment. Such critics point to the final act where Félix, the Roman governor, in his last-ditch effort to persuade his son-in-law to save his skin by recantation, offers the argument that, pardoned and free, Polyeucte may be able to use his influence and popularity to bring about some abatement in the persecution of his sect. But Polyeucte defiantly rejects the proposal and welcomes the arena and the lions.

> Non, non, persécutez,
> Et soyez l'instrument de nos félicités;
> Celle d'un vrai chrétien n'est que dans les souffrances;
> Les plus cruels tourments lui sont des récompenses.
> Dieu, qui rend le centuple aux bonnes actions,
> Pour comble donne encor les persécutions.[*]

The reason, however, for this outburst is that Polyeucte knows perfectly well that Félix is using arguments in which he does not believe. He is never going to allow his son-in-law to endanger his position with the emperor by engaging in pro-Christian propaganda, nor does he even wish to see the persecutions cease. Yet the forgiving Polyeucte, always interested in saving souls, even such a one as his father-in-law's, nonetheless assures him that, once in heaven, he will intervene with God on his behalf.

> Et c'est là que bientôt, voyant Dieu face à face,
> Plus aisément pour vous j'obtiendrai cette grâce.[†]

And the proof for me that Polyeucte, in the eyes of Corneille, is right in all that he says and does is that, immediately following his

---

[*]No, no, go on with your persecutions, and be the tool of our greater happiness. That for a true Christian lies in tortures; the very cruelest are pleasurable to him. God, who rewards good deeds a hundredfold, rewards us most with persecution.

[†]And there, soon, meeting God face to face, I shall the more easily obtain this grace for you.

execution, the promised grace is indeed accorded, and Félix, devious factor of evil that he is, is suddenly, as if struck by lightning from above, converted to the new faith. If the miracle is not accepted, the scene is ludicrous. The governor suddenly exclaims:

> Je m'y trouve forcé par un secret appas,
> Je cède à des transports que je ne connais pas;
> Et par un mouvement que je ne puis entendre,
> De ma fureur je passe au zèle de mon gendre.*

It has been noted that in the final scene of reconciliation between Fèlix, Sévère, and Pauline there is no mention of sadness over the death of Polyeucte, just minutes before. But Félix and Pauline, both now fully converted, are in awe before his martyrdom and presumable sainthood, and Sévère, more than half converted himself, is resolving to place all his credit with the emperor at risk to stop the persecutions. They seem to be seeing the deceased as sitting on the steps of the throne of God. The situation is beyond tears and lamentations.

And what of the Roman Empire in all of this? Insofar as it is represented by Sévère, it would seem to have been taken over by the new Christian spirit. Indeed, Sévère might offer the best of both rules, for he advocates freedom of worship and universal toleration, a spirit certainly not evidenced by Polyeucte and Néarque when they interrupt an official sacrifice to break up the statues of the gods. But the important thing in the play is that the imagery formerly used to describe the boundless power of the Roman Empire is now used to delineate the limitless domain of the Christian deity. Polyeucte states his creed:

> Je n'adore qu'un Dieu, maître de l'univers,
> Sous qui tremblent le ciel, la terre et les enfers;
> Un Dieu qui, nous aimant d'une amour infinie,
> Voulut mourir pour nous avec ignominie.†

---

*I find myself drawn by a secret appeal. I give way to transports which I don't recognize, and by some inner process that I fail to understand, I have passed from my madness to the religious zeal of my son-in-law.

†I adore but one God, lord of the universe, beneath whom tremble the earth, sky, and underworld, who, loving us with an infinite love, chose to die ignominiously on our behalf.

Théodore and *Pulchérie*

I put *Théodore* and *Pulchérie* together because they represent two termination points for Corneille in his treatment of the Roman Empire. *Théodore, vierge et martyre* is set in Antioch a few years after the death of Diocletian in 305 A.D., presumably in the reign of Maximin Daia (305–313), the Caesar under the second tetrarchy who ruled over Syria and was responsible for what was probably the last persecution of the Christians there. I doubt that Corneille regarded the Christian empire, shortly to be established by Constantine I, as a true part of the annals of Old Rome. And he certainly didn't think of the eastern empire of Byzantium, treated by him in *Pulchérie*, as that. It was too exotic, too bizarre. It had its time of glory, but its glory was of a different kind.

Théodore, like *Polyeucte,* deals with divine grace. Marcelle, wife of the Roman governor of Antioch and stepmother of his son, Placide, wants the latter for her adored daughter, Flavie, who is so madly in love with him that she will die if she cannot have him. But Placide is in love with Théodore and won't look at Flavie. So Marcelle, a woman of savage, even pathological, temper, willing to commit any crime to get her way and discovering that Théodore is a member of the outlawed Christian sect, arranges to have her abducted to a house of prostitution where, violated by soldiers, she will become an unfit bride for the man Marcelle wants for her daughter. Théodore, however, before she

73

is so stained, is rescued not by Placide but by Didyme, a Christian like herself and with whom she is in love, but who, unlike Placide, respects her determination to be a bride of Christ. Marcelle, now driven to near madness by her daughter's death (she has expired at last from unrequited love), contrives to capture both Théodore and Didyme, kills them and kills herself. The other characters, including Placide, comment nervously on the violent events that explode around them.

Théodore and Didyme supply such interest as this curious drama affords, illustrating what Corneille supposed to have been the fanatical zeal of the early Christians to be. The heroine admits to a strong attraction to Didyme, as opposed to Placide, but she is resolved to dedicate herself to Christ, and she is overjoyed to be condemned to death by the governor at his wife's instigation. What a perfect solution to the dilemma of heart and faith! But she is appalled when she learns what Marcelle's real plan for her is. Torture she would have welcomed, but not this! However, she soon decides that what is forced upon her cannot degrade her in the eyes of God, and she tells Placide, who wishes to save her by marriage and escape to Egypt, that she'd rather be raped and killed than go with him. One can imagine his humiliation. She tries to explain:

> Mais, seigneur, à ce mot ne soyez pas jaloux.
> Quelque haute splendeur que vous teniez de Rome,
> Il est plus grand que vous; mais ce n'est point un
>   homme:
> C'est le dieu des chrétiens, c'est le maître des rois,
> C'est lui qui tient ma foi, c'est lui dont j'ai fait choix;
> Et c'est enfin à lui que mes vœux ont donnée
> Cette virginité que l'on a condamnée.*

---

*But, sir, don't let this make you jealous. Whatever high rank you hold in Rome, he is greater than you. Nor is he even a man. He is the god of the Christians, the overlord of kings. It is he whom I worship, he whom I have chosen as my master, he to whom my vows have offered that virginity that your laws have condemned.

The play simply falls apart here. For if a martyr will suffer any torture with joy, is rape really so much worse than the rack or the fire? Théodore is superhuman; her trials cease to interest. Yet there is one curious twist in her thinking. When Didyme slips into her cell and offers to change clothes with her so that she can escape, leaving him to die in her place, she listens and ultimately accepts. His argument is that it behooves them both to save her viginity at the price of his coveted martyrdom. Speaking of himself in the third person he says:

> Une plus sainte ardeur règne au cœur de Didyme:
> Il vient de votre honneur se faire la victime,
> Le payer de son sang, et s'exposer pour vous
> A tout ce qu'oseront la haine et le courroux.
> Fuyez sous mon habit, et me laissez, de grâce,
> Sous le vôtre en ces lieux occuper votre place:
> C'est par ce moyen seul qu'on peut vous garantir:
> Conservez une vierge en faisant un martyr.[*]

"Dieu la persuade,"[†] he tells Placide later, and Théodore escapes to temporary safety. But when she learns that Flavie is dead and that Marcelle, rendered less vindictive by grief, seeks only her death now and not her rape, she emerges from hiding and attempts to take Didyme's place on the scaffold. Since his crime consisted in freeing her, her reappearance should clear him. But it seems that she actually envies him the martyrdom. When he resists, she pleads:

> Rends-moi, rends-moi ma place assez et trop gardée,
> Pour me sauver l'honneur je te l'avais cédée;
> Jusque-là seulement j'ai souffert ton secours;
> Mais je la viens reprendre alors qu'on veut mes jours.

---

[*]A holier ardor reigns in Didyme's heart; he comes to be the victim of your faith, to pay for it with his blood, to expose himself for your sake to all that hate and wrath can inflict upon him. Put on my clothes and flee, and leave me yours to take your place here. It's the only way you can be spared this horror. Save a virgin in making a martyr.

[†]God persuades her.

Rends, Didyme, rends-moi le seul bien où j'aspire,
C'est le droit de mourir, c'est l'honneur du martyre.
A quel titre peux-tu retenir mon bien?[*]

But Didyme demands to know what right has she to take it from *him*. Marcelle, listening to their impassioned debate, is outraged:

Donc jusques à ce point vous bravez ma colère,
Qu'en vous faisant périr je ne vous puis déplaire,
Et, que, loin de trembler sous la punition,
Vous y courez tous deux avec ambition![†]

She rapidly makes them both martyrs with her own knife and has the satisfaction of witnessing the agony of Placide, the real object of her hate, when he rushes in just in time to see his beloved Théodore expire. Marcelle reaches a satanic pinnacle of fury before turning her blade upon herself. The terrible scene, of course, must come to the audience through a witness.

Cependant, triomphante entre ces deux mourants,
Marcelle les contemple à ses pieds expirants,
Jouit de sa vengeance, et d'un regard avide
En cherche les douleurs jusqu'au cœur de Placide;
Et tantôt se repaît de leurs derniers soupirs,
Tantôt goûte à pleins yeux ses mortels déplaisirs,
Y mesure sa joie et trouve plus charmante
La douleur de l'amant que la mort de l'amante.[‡]

But of course Corneille and his audience knew that she was going straight to hell.

Pulchérie, like *Tite et Bérénice*, is a heroic comedy, as it ends neither with a murder nor a suicide. Its events unfold in the year

---

[*]Give me back my place which you have kept only too well. I ceded it to save my honor; for that only I accepted your help. But now I learn that they will be satisfied with my life. Give me back, Didyme, the only boon to which I aspire, the right to die, the glory of martyrdom. What right have you to keep it from me?

[†]You go this far in defying my wrath! I can't even displease you in killing you! And far from trembling at the prospect, you both rush to it!

[‡]Standing, however, triumphantly between her two expiring foes, Marcelle

450 A.D., just after the death of the young Byzantine emperor Theodosius II, for whom his older sister Pulcheria has been acting as regent for fifteen years. In history Pulcheria was fifty at the time, but Corneille represents her as considerably younger, though she must be at least in her late thirties, as the period of the regency is mentioned in the play. She is unmarried, and the senate has decreed that she must have a husband if she is to succeed her brother as sovereign. She faces the problem of love in the stalwart way of a Corneille political heroine. She favors the young Léon, but if he is not acceptable to the senate she will have none of him.

Hear her in the opening lines of the play:

Je vous aime, Léon, et n'en fais point mystère;
Des feux tels que les miens n'ont rien qu'il faille taire:
Je vous aime, et non point de cette folle ardeur,
Que les yeux éblouis font maîtresse du cœur.*

On the contrary, she assures him:

Ma passion pour vous, généreuse et solide,
A la vertu pour âme, et la raison pour guide.†

The senate has expressed its willingness to allow her the free choice of a husband, but so rigorous is her sense of duty that she cannot name Léon as her consort. He is brave and bright, she believes, but he is too young and untested, and his elevation would give rise to dangerous resentments and envy among his seniors in court. And indeed the samples of Byzantine courtiers to whom we are introduced show a dark and treacherous palace, very different (except in *Othon*) from the western Rome which was Corneille's concept of a great empire.

The play, as Voltaire pointed out, is cold, hopelessly cold.

---

exults in her vengeance, searching for agony in the features of the watching Placide, more ecstatic over the grief of the lover than over the death throes of his beloved.

*I love you, Leon, and make no secret of it. An ardor such as mine is nothing to be ashamed of; it's not one of those foolish crushes that dazzled eyes make the mistress of the heart.

†My feeling for you is generous and sure; it has virtue for soul and reason for guide.

There are no characters with whom we feel much sympathy. Léon is the palest hero in all of Corneille. He professes to adore Pulchérie for her person and not her throne, and there is no reason to disbelieve him, but his love is a weak, bloodless, self-pitying one; one almost despises him for it. He is constantly expressing his wish to die if he cannot wed Pulchérie, either as empress or not.

> J'y mourrais à vos yeux en adorant vos charmes;
> Peut-être essuieriez-vous quelqu'une de mes larmes;
> Peut-être ce grand cœur, qui n'ose s'attendrir,
> S'y défendrait si mal de mon dernier soupir,
> Qu'un éclat imprévu de douleur et de flamme
> Malgré vous à son tour voudrait suivre mon âme.[*]

Small wonder that she has doubts as to his qualifications to reign! And soon she begins to wonder if she would really have the independence needed to rule an empire married to any man, even the subservient Léon. She confesses to her confidant:

> Justine, plus j'y pense et plus je m'inquiète:
> Je crains de n'avoir plus une amour si parfaite,
> Et que, si de Léon on me fait un époux,
> Un bien si désiré ne me soit plus si doux.
> Je ne sais si le rang m'aurait fait changer d'âme;
> Mais je tremble à penser que je serais sa femme,
> Et qu'on n'épouse point l'amant le plus chéri
> Qu'on ne se fasse un maître aussitôt qu'un mari.[†]

I cannot repress a modern reaction to her apprehension. Léon strikes me as precisely the kind of sniveling self-dramatizer who

---

[*]I would die before your eyes in adoring your charms. Perhaps you would condescend to wipe away my tears. Perhaps that stout heart of yours, which eschews pity, would be so overcome by my last sighs that an irrepressible burst of emotion would in spite of yourself make you wish to follow my spirit.

[†]Justine, the more I think of this, the more it worries me. I'm afraid that Leon's and my love may not be quite what I had hoped and that if they appoint him to be my husband, things may not go quite as I have wished. I don't know that the rank would change his disposition, but I tremble to think that I would be his wife and that in marrying even the dearest lover one gives oneself a master as well as a spouse.

would seek to dominate any woman ruler who was fool enough to marry him. But this was surely not Corneille's idea of his hero.

The characters who solve the problem of Pulchérie and Léon are Martian, the famous old army hero who for a decade has silently loved the empress, and his daughter, Justine, who silently loves Léon. Father and daughter discuss their common frustration in a dialogue that could occur only in a play by Corneille. Madame de Sévigné found her favorite tragedian tender and moving on the subject of an old man's love (believed by some to have been inspired by Corneille's passion for a young actress), but I cannot help but find almost senile a national hero's statement to his own child that he hopes to expire on the day that Pulchérie weds another man. Yet when he offers the same prognostication to the empress herself, he does so in one of the few passages of the play that is as fine as in any of Corneille's major works:

> Dans cet heureux moment qu'il sera votre époux,
> J'abandonne Byzance et prends congé de vous,
> Pour aller, dans le calme et dans la solitude,
> De la mort qui m'attend faire la heureuse étude.[*]

And this may be the place to cite another verse that might have been taken from the maxims of La Rochefoucauld:

> Pour l'intérêt public rarement on soupire,
> Si quelque ennui secret n'y mêle son martyre.[†]

Pulchérie's somewhat grotesque solution is to marry Martian under condition that theirs shall be a union in name only—her chastity must be sacredly preserved. As to Léon, he will be married off to Martian's daughter with a good chance of inheriting the empire, since obviously no issue are to be expected from the imperial match. The play may be a comedy to us, but is it really a heroic one? We can admit anyway that Pulchérie is loyal to her resolution:

---

[*]On that happy day when he becomes your husband I shall bid farewell to Byzantium and take my leave of you to devote myself, in calmness and solitude, to a serene contemplation of the death that awaits me.

[†]We rarely sigh over misfortunes of state when a private woe is not mixed up with them.

Et jalouse déjà de mon pouvoir suprême,
Pour l'affermir sur tous, je le prends sur moi-même.[*]

But has it been as difficult for her as our author suggests? We may doubt it.

Corneille had written one earlier tragedy about the Byzantine empire, *Héraclius*, which is concerned with events in the reign of the usurping and eventually assassinated emperor Phocas, 602–610 A.D., but the plot, dealing with a series of babies substituted in imperial cradles, is of such complication that Gibbon in a footnote in his *History of the Decline and Fall of the Roman Empire* describes it as one "which requires more than one representation to be clearly understood and which after an interval of some years is said to have puzzled the author himself." It was felt that a consideration of it would add little to this study.

---

[*]And already jealous of my supreme power, to confirm it on all, I bow to it myself.

Attila

The action of *Attila*, which, as in all classic tragedy, is limited to a single place and day, occurs in the camp of the King of the Huns in Illyria, 452 A.D., in the last twenty-four hours of his life. The same number of years, twenty-four, remained for the doomed western empire of Rome, although the eastern would survive for another millennium. The final division of the whole between the two sons of Theodosius the Great had been made on his death in 395, the west going to Honorius and the east to Arcadius. Corneille, after *Attila,* would no longer be concerned with the death rattle of the former.

Attila, the "Scourge of God," had overwhelmed the bulk of Europe, including such former barbarian foes of Rome as the Gepides and the Ostrogoths, and he was now poised between the two cowering Roman emperors, undecided as to which to engulf first. Unlike the tyrants of our own day, he represented no political, social, or religious theory; he reddened the map with blood simply to satisfy his own lust for power. He would sack city after city, slaughtering the inhabitants except for such as would make useful slaves or enlistable soldiers. He loomed before the terrified peoples of Europe and the Mideast as the end of civilization, perhaps the end of the known world itself.

The concise and brilliant couplets of Corneille, like the rolling and sonorous sentences of Gibbon, seem to imprison the dreary history of this time in a golden gridiron of beauty, giving the

81

reader the needed sense that something, after all, has survived an age of hopelessness. Let us take Gibbon first:

"In the reign of Attila the Huns again became the terror of the world; and I shall now describe the character and actions of that formidable barbarian, who alternately insulted and invaded the East and the West, and urged the rapid downfall of the Roman empire. . . . His features, according to the observation of a Gothic historian, bore the stamp of his national origin; and the portrait of Attila exhibits the genuine deformity of a modern Calmuck; a large head, a swarthy complexion, small deep-seated eyes, a flat nose, a few hairs in the place of a beard, broad shoulders and a short square body, of nervous strength, though of a disproportioned form. The haughty step and demeanor of the king of the Huns expressed the consciousness of his superiority over the rest of mankind, and he had a custom of fiercely rolling his eyes, as if he wished to enjoy the terror which he inspired."

His captive kings survived only to be treated as his servants: "They watched his nod; they trembled at his frown; and at the first signal of his will, they executed, without murmur or hesitation, his stern and absolute commands."

Yet he rarely allowed his wrath to prevail over his judgment: "He delighted in war; but after he had ascended the throne in a mature age, his head rather than his hand achieved the conquest of the North, and the fame of an adventurous soldier was usefully exchanged for that of a prudent and successful general."

Corneille makes the same point:

> Il aime à conquérir, mais il hait les batailles:
> Il veut que son nom seul renverse les murailles;
> Et plus grand politique encore que grand guerrier,
> Il tient que les combats sentent l'aventurier.*

As Corneille's play opens, Attila is debating which of the two princesses whom he has summoned to his camp will he wed: Honorie, the haughty sister of the western emperor Valentian III,

---

*He loves to conquer, but he hates battles; he wants the fortifications to tumble before his name. He's an even greater politician than warrior, and feels that a preference for combat smacks of the adventurer.

who claims to share the imperium with her weak and feckless brother, or Ildione, sister of the glorious king of the Francs, whom Corneille, in a cringingly flattering and utterly irrelevant speech in the play, likens to the young Louis XIV. The princesses, unbeknownst to Attila, are in love with two of his captive kings: Honorie with Valamir, king of the Ostrogoths, and Ildione with Ardaric, king of the Gepides. Yet each woman is patriotic and willing, even eager, to wed the despised Attila in the political interests of her country.

Attila's opening lines set the mood of the tragedy:

> Ils ne sont pas venus, nos deux rois? Qu'on leur die
> Qu'ils se font trop attendre, et qu'Attila s'ennuie;
> Qu'alors que je les mande, ils doivent se hâter.*

The drama of the play will lie in the tenseness of the cruel cat-and-mouse games that the tyrant plays with his four captives as he learns of the inner state of their affairs. He holds all the cards but one: he has fallen in love with Ildione, very much against his will, for the Roman lady represents the more advantageous political match. The picture of the Hun in love may be a bit out of focus, but there is something almost pathetic in his furious and desperate appeal to Ildione to renounce him of her own accord, so as to avoid an international incident:

> Quoi? vous pourriez m'aimer, Madame, à votre tour?
> Qui sème tant d'horreurs fait naître peu d'amour.
> Qu'aimeriez-vous en moi? Je suis cruel, barbare,
> Je n'ai que ma fierté, que ma fureur de rare
> On me craint, on me hait, on me nomme en tout lieu
> La terreur des mortels et le fléau de Dieu.†

In history Ildione actually married Attila and has been credited by some historians with murdering him on their wedding night.

---

*They haven't come yet, our two kings? Tell them they're making me wait and that bores me. When I send for them, they'd better jump.

†What, madam? You could love me? The man who spreads the devastation that I have is not apt to arouse much love. What could you love in me? I am cruel, barbaric; I have nothing but my pride and fury. I am feared and hated and known throughout the world as the terror of man and the scourge of God.

But in the play, a lovely, noble-spirited, and very royal princess, she is spared any such match and fate by the tyrant's premature death from a massive hemorrhage. Honorie is less sympathetically drawn, though she is considerably finer than she was in history, where she is supposed to have borne a child to her steward and plotted to marry Attila with an eye to deposing her brother.

Honorie, indeed, is the most subtly depicted character in the drama. She epitomizes all that is still proud and noble in a decadent empire. She has lofty bearing and lofty thoughts as to her own position, but her pride is closer to vanity, and she is weakly and impetuously foolish when she should be cool and diplomatic. The best scene in the play is the one in which she rejects the marriage proposal that she has sought from Attila upon discovering that he has obliged Ildione, whom he truly loves, to give him up. Honorie will not accept a hand, even that of the lord of the world, from the hand of a social inferior. A dying Rome has at least this to offer:

> Le débris de l'empire a de belles ruines:
> S'il n'a plus de héros, il a des héroïnes.[*]

Honorie's pride becomes for the moment almost her *gloire*:

> Et ce n'est pas ainsi qu'il plaît qu'on use:
> Je cesse d'estimer ce qu'une autre refuse,
> Et bien que vos traités vous engagent ma foi,
> Le rebut d'Ildione est indigne de moi.
> Oui, bien que l'univers ou vous serve ou vous craigne,
> Je n'ai que des mépris pour ce qu'elle dédaigne.[†]

But then she spoils it all, which is just what we have suspected she will do. She stupidly reveals to Attila that she loves Valamir and demonstrates a shrill spite in begging him not to let Ildione

---

[*]The debris of an empire makes still for fine ruins; if the heroes are gone, the heroines remain.

[†]It is not thus that I wish to be used. I cease to value what another has rejected. And even though the treaties assure you of my compliance, what Ildione won't have is not worthy of me. Oh, yes, however much the universe may serve or fear you, I disdain what she has disdained.

wed her lover Ardaric. If Honorie can't be happy herself, she doesn't want anyone else to be. Perhaps the Rome she represents wasn't worth saving.

Attila resents Ardaric and Valamir, not only because they have had the presumption to court secretly his two candidate princesses, but also because they have dared to consider themselves, even as captive sovereigns, his equals. In this Corneille may be showing himself more concerned with his own century, where rank was everything, than with the fifth, where power alone counted. In the age of the Sun King to have a territory of which one was sovereign, even if it was only a few acres of land, and even if one had lost it, made one rank equally with every monarch in Europe. That was why the Princesse des Ursins, all-powerful lady-in-waiting to the queen of Spain, was always begging Louis XIV, whose international policies she was paid to support in Madrid, to give her, as part of her compensation, some tiny territory to rule. She did not obtain her wish.

Attila at the end of the play causes the two kings to be disarmed and treats them as gladiators. The one who succeeds in killing the other will have his life spared. Of course, they spurn him. *Gloire* can be found now only in death. As Ardaric puts it:

> Il est beau de périr pour éviter un crime:
> Quand on meurt pour sa gloire, on revit dans l'estime
> Et triompher ainsi du plus rigoureux sort
> C'est s'immortaliser par une illustre mort.[*]

Attila will now marry Ildione, who again offers herself as the price of her lover's life, though one doesn't for a minute believe that he will spare either Ardaric or Valamir. And into the bargain he will humiliate the proud Honorie by giving her to the captain of his guard. He now reveals himself as literally the scourge of a deity who plans to destroy the world:

> Ce dieu dont vous parlez, de temps en temps sévère,
> Ne s'arme pas toujours de toute sa colère;

---

[*]It's a fine thing to die to avoid a crime. When one dies for one's glory, one lives on in the public esteem. To triumph over a harsh fate is to immortalize oneself in a noble death.

Mais quand à sa fureur il livre l'univers,
Elle a pour chaque temps des déluges divers.
Jadis, de toutes parts faisant regorger l'onde,
Sous un déluge d'eaux il abîma le monde;
Sa main tient en réserve un déluge de feux
Pour le dernier moment de nos derniers neveux;
Et mon bras, dont il fait aujourd'hui son tonnerre,
D'un déluge de sang couvre pour lui la terre.*

But it will be his own blood that will cover him, off stage, of course, for a protagonist could hardly die before the eyes of a classical audience of a torrential nosebleed. It is another case in Corneille of the use of the Greek deus ex machina, but there was no other way in which he could resolve his drama, as everyone in the pit and boxes knew the fate of the king of the Huns.

---

*This god of whom you speak, who can be harsh on occasion, does not avail himself at all times of the full vent of his wrath, but when he does he has different devastations for different times. Once he drowned the world in a flood. But for the final destruction of his last creations he has reserved a deluge of fire and my arm to sound his thunder and cover the earth with blood.

Suréna

T he tragedies of Corneille which deal with the Roman Empire
have been taken up in the chronological order of the eras
depicted rather than in the sequence of their composition, but I
reserve a final chapter for *Suréna*, the last written of the poet's
dramas but one whose action lies in the aftermath of the Parthian
defeat of Marcus Licinius Crassus in 53 B.C. Surena, the Parthian
general, not only overthrew the Roman legions at Carrhai and
slew their commander; he established Orode, his own monarch,
as the greatest potentate of the Mideast, thereby sealing his own
doom in the heart of that jealous ruler who could not conceive
that so valiant a subordinate could be permanently loyal to him.
The play is not primarily concerned with the story of Rome, but
as it constitutes its author's final comment on heroism and *gloire*,
so long associated in his mind with the grandeur of the Latin
empire, it warrants some discussion here.

Suréna is more a poem than a play; it is too static to be
performed effectively, but it is beautiful to read. One feels from
the start that the hero is doomed by his cruel and unreasonable
foes and that he will accept his fate with a noble and stoical
resignation. Perhaps too much so. He seems at moments almost
too cool, too serene and accepting, too willing, as he puts it, to
see life as thwarted love, suffering, and death, even too compas-
sionate with the two unhappy women, his beloved Eurydice and
his sister Palmis, who seek wildly but clumsily to save him. Yet to

87

me he is the most sympathetic of Corneille's heroes, for he has charm and even gentleness and none of the prickly egotism which mars, even when it humanizes, so many of the warriors of seventeenth-century drama.

Every character in the play, whether loving or hostile to the hero, contributes, directly or indirectly, to his misery and downfall. Orode, the Parthian king, who owes his crown to Suréna and who has endangered even that by the unpopular proposed match between his son Pacorus and the princess of Parthian-defeated Armenia, Eurydice (the secret beloved of Suréna), plots to neutralize his all-powerful general either by assassination or by securing his unjustly suspected loyalty by marrying him to his daughter Mandane. Pacorus, his odious but clever and manipulating heir, willingly casts aside his old love, Palmis, Suréna's sister, to comply with his father's order to wed Eurydice, not so much for the highly dubious advantages of the alliance as to spite Eurydice for having a secret love. And when Pacorus discovers that this secret love is none other than the great hero of his national army, his meanness knows no bounds.

Suréna's allies, his beloved and his sister, are little help. Eurydice has all the virtues and faults of a Corneille heroine. Although her love for Suréna is absolute (she will literally die of it in the end) she is able to bring herself to comply with her father's order and do her duty as a princess by giving her hand to Pacorus, but she manages to do it in so taunting and provocative a way as to make the latter determined to punish her in any way he can. And although she is willing to see Suréna make a diplomatic marriage to ensure the siring of other warriors of his mettle, she forbids him to marry Mandane (simply, presumably, because Mandane, who never appears on stage and whom Suréna doesn't even know, is the sister of the despised Pacorus), which is the only way Suréna can save his own skin. She and Palmis indulge in a typical Corneille female argument as to which has the most to lose in the death of Suréna: the sister or the beloved. And between them they manage indiscreetly to let the cat of Eurydice's secret love out of the bag. After that there is no chance for Suréna to execute his own rescue plan, as both Orode and Pacorus are united in their opposition to a match between the daughter of the Armenian king and the great general. To guard against that at all costs Suréna must marry either Mandane or some other Parthian woman.

Suréna's plan of escape is a simple one. It is to endeavor to persuade Orode that the Armenian match is politically undesirable and that if it is broken off he, Suréna, will pacify the Armenians. Presumably he will do so by marrying the princess Eurydice himself. Then Pacorus can go back to his old love, Palmis, of whom he is still sufficiently fond (he only liked Eurydice out of pique) and that match will guarantee Suréna's loyalty to the Parthian crown as the future king will presumably be his own nephew. As for himself, he cannot not marry Mandane because he is not of royal blood.

Now Suréna is not being altogether sincere in this. Indeed, some French critics have raised the question as to whether he is acting quite as a tragic hero should. For his refusal to marry Mandane is not because she is of royal blood; Eurydice is royal as well. And maybe, according to such critics, it was his duty as a subject to marry Mandane and save the state from the military ruin which indeed followed his own assassination. That the king was unreasonably, even hysterically, jealous of his great officer was not the point; the point was that such was the way the king was and they all had to live with it. If the royal jealousy could be allayed, was it not the duty of a patriot to allay it? But Corneille was saying here something new about patriotism and the hero. Suréna has come to see his own integrity—part of which was to maintain his hand and heart free from any woman save the one he would always love—as something that was too precious to be surrendered even for the good of the state. In a darkling world it was a small solitary light that could only be extinguished by death.

There was also in his final reasoning a note of pessimism as to whether even a marriage to Mandane would save him. As he says to Eurydice:

> Madame, ce refus n'est pas vers lui mon crime;
> Vous m'aimez; ce n'est point non plus ce qui l'anime.

Mon crime véritable est d'avoir aujourd'hui
Plus de nom que mon roi, plus de vertu que lui;
Et c'est de là que part cette secrète haine
Que le temps ne rendra que plus forte et plus pleine.*

His last comments on his country and what he might accomplish on its behalf are desolate indeed. To Eurydice's plea that he should marry to generate heroic offspring he replies:

Que tout meure avec moi, Madame; que m'importe
Qui foule après ma mort la terre qui me porte?
Sentiront-ils percer par un éclat nouveau,
Ces illustres aïeux, la nuit de leur tombeau?
Respireront-ils l'air où les feront revivre
Ces neveux qui peut-être auront peine à les suivre,
Peut-être ne feront que les déshonorer,
Et n'en auront le sang que pour dégénérer?†

And he offers a final comment on the sovereign who has sought to enslave his heart and destroy his body.

Je lui dois en sujet tout mon sang, tout mon bien;
Mais si je lui dois tout, mon cœur ne lui doit rien,
Et n'en reçoit de lois que comme autant d'outrages,
Comme autant d'attentats sur de plus doux hommages.‡

We have come a long way from the blind patriotism of Horace.

---

*Madam, it isn't the refusal that's my crime, or even the fact that you love me. My real crime is to have a greater name and a keener sense of honor than my sovereign. That is the true source of his secret hate which time can only amplify.

†Let everything else die with me, madam. What does it matter who treads the earth after my death? Will my illustrious forebears be hallowed by any new light in the darkness of their tomb? Perhaps my descendants will hardly live up to them; maybe they will even dishonor them; perhaps they will inherit the blood only to have the stock degenerate.

‡As a subject I owe him my life and my worldly goods, but if *I* owe him all, my heart owes him naught, and I receive his commands as so many outrages, as so many rebuffs of the humblest homage.